Huxley's House of Plants

Huxley's House of Plants

•

Alyson and Anthony Huxley

PADDINGTON PRESS LTD
NEW YORK & LONDON

Library of Congress Cataloging in Publication Data

Huxley, Alyson, 1949–
Huxley's House of Plants.

Includes index.
1. House plants. 2. House plants in interior decoration. I. Huxley, Anthony Julian, 1920– joint author. II. Title. III. Title: House of plants.
SB419.H87 635.9'65 77–20976
ISBN 0–448–22422–4

Filmset by Photoprint Plates, Rayleigh, England
Produced by Mohn-Gordon Limited, London, and printed in Italy by Istituto Italiano D'Arti Grafiche S.P.A. Bergamo

IN THE UNITED STATES
PADDINGTON PRESS
Distributed by
GROSSET & DUNLAP

IN THE UNITED KINGDOM
PADDINGTON PRESS LTD.

IN CANADA
Distributed by
RANDOM HOUSE OF CANADA LTD.

IN SOUTHERN AFRICA
Distributed by
ERNEST STANTON (PUBLISHERS) (PTY.) LTD.

Introduction

There's something in most of us which needs greenery around. Today, more than ever, house plants have become an integral part of our lives. Particularly for those living in apartments perched high above paved streets, plants are one way of getting back in touch with nature. We ourselves would not dream of living in a house that was not full of plants—it just wouldn't feel like a home to us.

There's a difference between appreciating the very special touch plants add to a room and actually being able to grow them successfully in your own home. Some people are blessed with "green thumbs": they can cope with plants instinctively, knowing just when to water and feed them, sensing if there are problems, and finding just the right spots for them. Most people do not have this "feel," however, and it's with those of you who don't that we'd like to share the knowledge we've gained in building up our own HOUSE OF PLANTS.

First, in "From the Roots Up," we look briefly at how plants work and live. It's much easier to look after them if you understand something of this. Next, in "The ABZ of Plant Care," we set out the general procedure for looking after plants and examine the basic problems they face in the home.

The home is, after all, a quite unnatural environment for your plants. The important thing to realize is that no matter how much care and attention you lavish on them, you're bound for disaster if you don't take into account the special environment that each plant needs. Some will enjoy a sunny window, others a shady corner; some will thrive in a hot, dry atmosphere like your living room, others in a cooler, moister atmosphere such as that offered by a bathroom. The section "A Home with Plants in Mind" deals with all the subtleties of matching plant to place. Room by room, we take you on a guided tour of your home, giving you hints on how to analyze the particular environment and function of each room and how to choose plants that will thrive there and also help to beautify.

We've incorporated decorating ideas galore for you to help you develop a sense of artistry in potting and placing your plants. Special projects have also been included, with step-by-step pictures showing you how to make a moss pole for climbers and an intriguing bottle garden. We mention, too, unusual exotics like bromeliads and orchids, and many of the "special" groups like African violets, cacti and succulents, ferns, and bulbs. There's also a section on the art of propagating new plants from old, and one on how to grow unusual plants from left-overs like date and orange pits, peanuts, and sweet potatoes. And last but not least, there's a section on how to deal with trouble if it comes.

In short, we've tried to include everything you need to bring nature indoors and create your own very special HOUSE OF PLANTS.

Contents

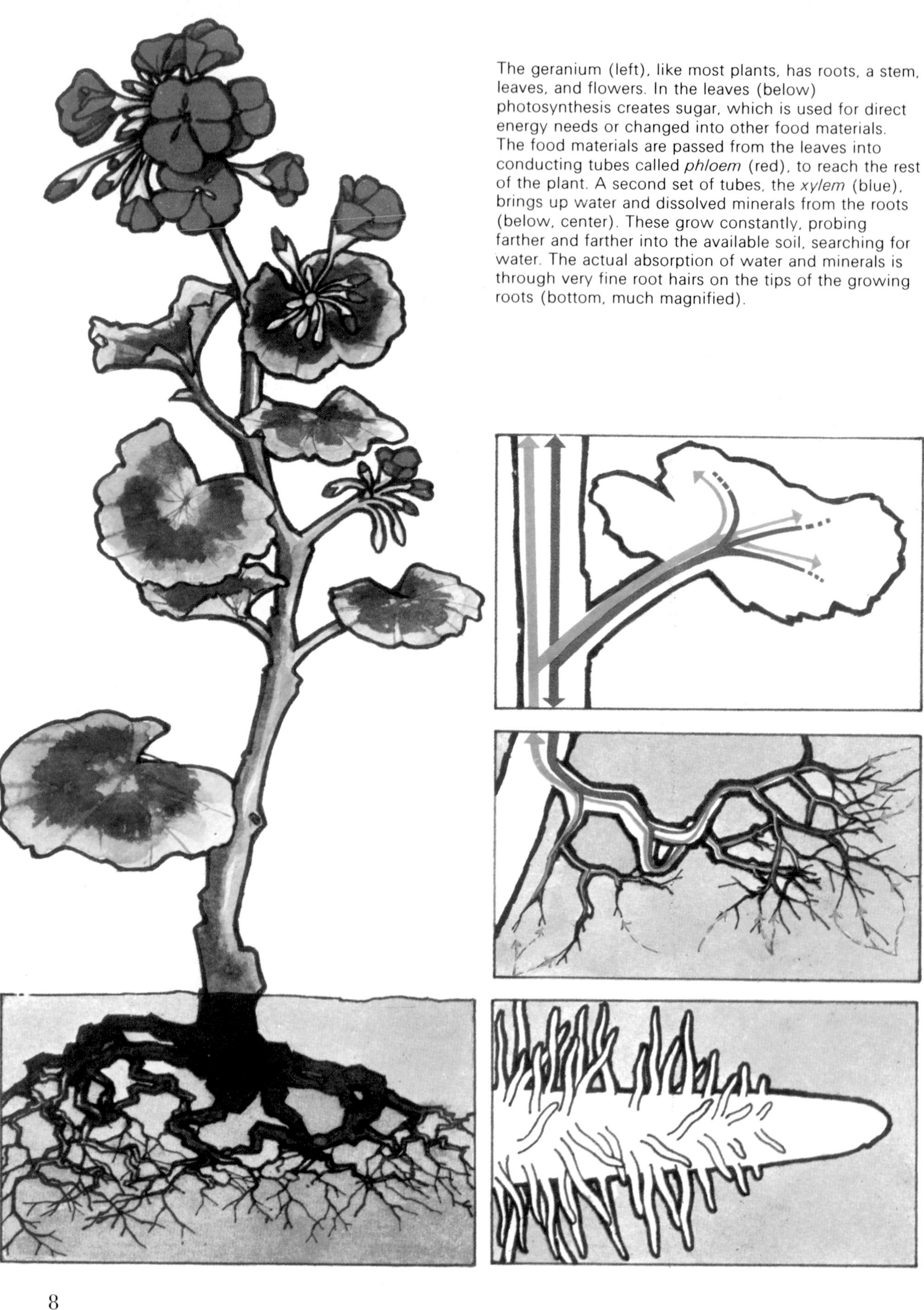

The geranium (left), like most plants, has roots, a stem, leaves, and flowers. In the leaves (below) photosynthesis creates sugar, which is used for direct energy needs or changed into other food materials. The food materials are passed from the leaves into conducting tubes called *phloem* (red), to reach the rest of the plant. A second set of tubes, the *xylem* (blue), brings up water and dissolved minerals from the roots (below, center). These grow constantly, probing farther and farther into the available soil, searching for water. The actual absorption of water and minerals is through very fine root hairs on the tips of the growing roots (bottom, much magnified).

From the Roots Up

Before we start indoor gardening it's a good idea to know something about how plants function, especially since in our homes we are growing them in unnatural conditions. Not only do we grow them in pots, which is certainly not how they grow in nature, but also we may find that in a single room we may be trying to grow several plants from very different kinds of environment. Plants are collected from all over the world to grow as house plants: from temperate regions and hot equatorial ones, from dry exposed deserts and humid tropical forests. So, knowing the sort of conditions they lived under originally will help us grow them in our homes.

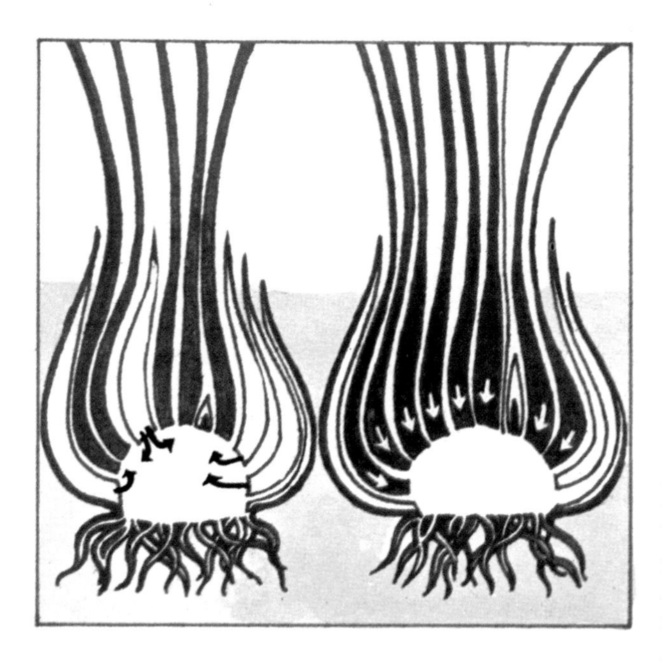

Above: Bulbs are storage organs from which, as leaves develop, food reserves are used (left). During the growing season, food manufactured in the leaves replenishes the store (right).

Let's start by looking at a typical plant, the one popularly called a geranium, say. Each of its parts, roots, stem, leaves, and—one of the main reasons for buying this particular one in the first place—flowers, have a definite function in the plant's life. The roots anchor the plant and absorb water and dissolved minerals. The stem lifts the plant above the ground and supports the leaves, which are the plant's energy factories.

To survive, a plant must be able to manufacture its own food. It does this with the aid of the green pigment *chlorophyll*, which is unique to plants and usually found concentrated in the leaves. Chlorophyll absorbs energy from the sun or other light source and uses it to combine water and carbon dioxide into a simple sugar called glucose. As a by-product, oxygen gas is released into the air. The whole of this operation is called *photosynthesis*, "putting together by light." The glucose is used by the plant to make new cells or is changed into starch and stored for future use. Other chemical changes convert glucose into oils, proteins and, in fact, all the substances found in plants.

Strangely, everything the plant does in photosynthesis it appears to undo in another operation called *respiration*, which is mainly carried out at night, when photosynthesis has to stop. During respiration the plant uses oxygen to turn sugar into the energy it needs to continue growing. The waste product of this operation is carbon dioxide that is released into the air from the plant's leaves. These gases, oxygen and carbon dioxide, pass in and out of the leaves through minute pores called *stomata*, which in most plants cover the underside of the leaves.

Right: A close-up look at a typical green leaf, the food factory of a plant. During the daytime sunlight absorbed by the green pigment chlorophyll energizes the process of photosynthesis in which carbon dioxide and water combine to produce the food substance glucose and the by-product oxygen. The process is reversed mainly at night as the energy locked up in glucose and food stores, such as starch, is released during respiration, which uses oxygen and produces carbon dioxide.
Inset: A magnified view of the leaf's internal structure. Layers of flat cells sandwich a "filling" of spongy cells that contain chlorophyll in disklike concentrations. The "plumbing" system of veins consists of xylem to bring water (blue) from roots to leaves and phloem to take food (red) to other parts of the plant. Pores, or stomata, occur mainly on the lower surface and allow evaporation of water and gaseous exchange (orange).

Most leaves turn themselves on a kind of joint at the bottom of the leaf stalk to expose the maximum surface to whatever light there is—that's why they face the window instead of into the room as we'd prefer. But, as well as catching the light plants need, leaves also present a large surface for evaporation of water. Drying winds, high temperatures, dry air all help to speed up the rate at which water is lost through the stomata on the leaves. This constant evaporation of water from the plant "draws" water up through the roots. Luckily the upper surfaces of most plant leaves are coated with a waxy material that slows up the rate of evaporation. As you'll see later on when we discuss various plants, some are better at retaining water than others. This is important in judging how much water to give your plants and how often they should be watered.

Although a plant can live on the glucose manufactured in the leaves and water, it needs minerals, too, for balanced growth. The minerals, or nutrients, are obtained from the soil, or from the fertilizers we add to potting mixtures. The water the plants need—and the nutrients dissolved in it—is taken up through the fine "hairs" on the root tips. The water and dissolved nutrients travel all over the plant through a system of tube-forming cells called the *xylem*. Another set of tubes, the *phloem*, passes glucose made in the leaves to all parts of the plant.

The flowers on some house plants are the reproductive organs. Their brilliant colors and sweet fragrance, which we prize so much, are really to attract the insects that help pollinate them. Once on the flower, the insects feed on the nectar and pollen produced there. The pollen from the male parts of the flower (stamens) sticks onto the insect's body and is rubbed off onto the female part of the flower (stigma). The seeds are made fertile and fruits are formed. There's not much opportunity for insects to get into our homes to the flowers and generally it doesn't matter—many plants can be reproduced in other ways which we will discuss under "Increasing Your Stock" (pages 122–129). Most plants, in any case, are quite difficult to raise from seed without a greenhouse.

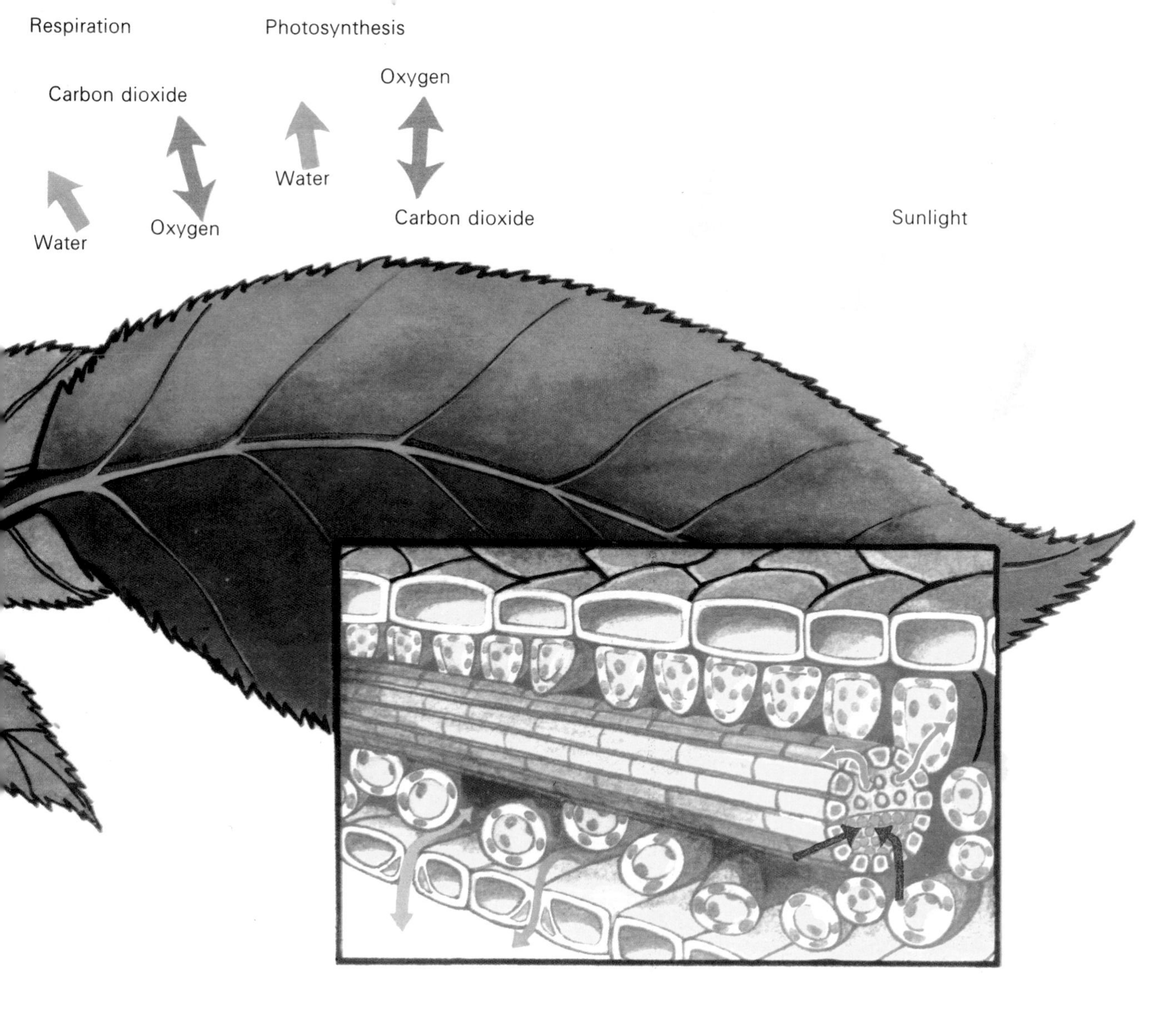

If you are growing fruit trees for ornament indoors and you want to be certain that fruit forms, you will have to play the part of the pollinating insect yourself. All you do is take a fine paint brush—the sort used for watercolor painting—and gently dust pollen from the stamens of one of the flowers on your tree onto the stigma of another.

How the plant supports itself depends largely on its size. Most large plants, the shrubs or trees, have woody stems for support. Plants that aren't woody, but whose stems are green and soft, are termed herbaceous. Trees, shrubs, and many herbaceous plants live from year to year and are known as perennials. It is from among these plants that most house plants are chosen. Many other herbaceous plants grow anew every year from seed. They flower, produce more seed, and then die within a year. They are known as annuals and are generally used to provide seasonal splashes of color in outdoor gardens, though some annuals grown for greenhouse decoration can also be used indoors.

Many people talk to their plants and claim it makes them grow better. Whether the plants grow better because they're talked to, or because the owners who talk to them are more sensitive to the needs of their plants, is something you can decide for yourself. What is important, though, is to keep in mind that each type of plant requires a special combination of water, light, air, and food. Then it's much easier to realize why they may thrive or not in a place that is, after all, very foreign indeed to their nature.

Baby Bio
POTTING
Compost
Garden Peat
double action
*makes heavy soils easier to work
*maintains moisture in light soils
COMPOST
better & easier
plants & seedlings
7lbs
NET WEIGHT
JOHN
INNES
No.2
COMPOST
MIXED & PACKED BY—STUART LOW CO. (Enfield) LIMITED
3 LB NET

The ABZ of Plant Care

When you next go to your garden shop, nursery, or plant boutique to buy a new house plant, you'll notice that they mostly come in plastic pots. This is mainly because they are easier for shops and stores—and for you—to handle and package than the clay ones. Plastic pots are lighter in weight and don't break so easily if dropped. They are popular too, because you can buy plastic pots in many colors, which may fit in better with your color scheme at home.

The advantages are not all with plastic, though. You may well prefer a clay pot, particularly for your larger plants. As clay is heavier than plastic, the pot won't topple over so readily if your plant gets top-heavy. Also, like many people, you may decide clay has a much more earthy and naturally pleasing look than plastic.

When it comes to watering your plants, both types of pot have their advantages. You'll notice that plastic pots have a number of small holes in the bottom instead of the single large one in a clay pot. The extra holes help the pot to drain well. Clay pots, on the other hand, are porous. Plants are not so likely to become waterlogged because the clay absorbs and evaporates any excess water that the plant cannot drink.

Be warned: kindness can kill! Nowhere is this truer than when it comes to watering—or rather overwatering—house plants. Many new house-plant gardeners tend to give their plants a daily "splash" of water so that the potting mix doesn't dry out: the sad result is usually a soggy mass of soil in which the oxygen-starved roots rot.

Left: Some items for successful plant growing: potting mixes, fertilizers, plant pots and tray, water pot, mist sprayer, leaf shine, dusting brush, self-watering mat, plastic bags, thermometer plus hygrometer (to register humidity), and a soil moisture meter.

So what is the right amount of water to give your plants? Well, that will depend on the type of plant, how big it is, where it is—in a bathroom, a kitchen, on the patio, and so on—and the time of year. You can't water by rules. A plant needs watering when the soil has become a bit on the dry side—don't let it dry out completely or the plant will begin to wilt—just as it will if it's overwatered too! You'll soon learn to distinguish between dry and moist soil—be guided by the look, feel, and smell of it. Dry soil is hard and looks grayish in color. The right kind of texture is when the moist soil is dark and sticks to your fingers when you press them lightly into it—the soil has a pastry-crumb texture and a rich, earthy smell.

If you're not certain of the difference between nicely moist and wet soil then get yourself a moisture meter, which will let you see at a glance when to water. The meter is usually scaled in three sections, wet–moist–dry, but sometimes in numbers; the handbook that comes packaged with the meter will give you all the necessary details for accurate use.

You'll find a watering pot with a long narrow spout a good investment. You can then direct water at exactly the right place, which could be into a small pot or among compact foliage. With your more delicate plants it is a good idea to let water stand at room temperature for a while before watering. Cold water directly from the faucet is too chilly for some plants and may make some of the leaves drop off. Rainwater is even

Above: There are two kinds of plant pot—clay and plastic. Clay pots have been used for thousands of years: they have a single drainage hole, are heavy and porous, and allow excess water to evaporate. Plastic pots have several drainage holes, are much lighter, and don't let water escape through the sides, so plants need watering less often.

Below: Although watering eventually becomes instinctive, a moisture meter will tell you at a glance when to water. This model measures the electrical conductivity of the soil, which increases with moisture content, and displays the result with a needle on a numbered scale.

better, of course, and won't leave the ugly, whitish deposit on the soil that may come from a hard domestic water supply; but take care in areas where it may be polluted.

If you find you've overlooked watering one of your plants, so that it wilts or flags, the remedy is simple—put it into a bucket or sink of water until the air bubbles stop coming up. Then let it drain. Waterlogged plants, on the other hand, must be allowed to dry out almost completely, but they may not recover if the roots have rotted.

Plants must have a certain range of temperature and light to flourish properly; we will give the actual level each needs later on when we discuss individual plants. Although some plants may like it hot, and others cool, they all prefer a fairly *constant* air temperature. They will tolerate some variation, of course, but be warned: any drastic change in conditions can be fatal.

For instance, plants arranged on windowsills will suffer in cold weather, perhaps eventually losing leaves, if they're left behind curtains and so insulated from the warmth of the room. Windowsills are trouble spots in summer, too. The temperature by the window can then be several degrees higher than the rest of the room, and your plants can suffer. Other spots to watch for are radiators and air-conditioning outlets.

Most of our homes have some form of heating system. This is fine for us, but do remember that house plants are affected by a very dry atmosphere. Unless you're concentrating on growing cacti or succulents, which love dry air, you'll have to provide your plants with some form of humidity or else they will rapidly become discolored, shrivel, and gradually lose their leaves.

The really all-important "invisible" factor in successful house-plant growing is getting the correct amount of air humidity. There are several ways of making sure that your plants get all the humid air they need to remain healthy and beautiful. The simplest is to stand the pot in a dish or tray of gravel or pebbles and add water, so that the stones

Above: The great enemy of plants is dry air—impossible to see or feel, though a hygrometer will measure it. One way of providing extra air humidity is to use a mist sprayer.

are nearly covered but the water does not reach the bottom of the pot. The evaporating water will give your plants all the humidity they need and there's the added advantage that you can tell at a glance when more water is needed.

Another way is to push the pot into a container of damp peat or moss (remember to water it as well as the plant, to keep it moist). These methods work even better when you have several plants you want to group together. Simply arrange all of the plants you want to group on a big pebble tray, or in a deep-sided container filled with peat, which will not be very noticeable with plants trailing over the edges. The water evaporated from below, as well as the vapor given off by the plants as they "breathe," make a sort of invisible cloud around the entire grouping and helps every plant in it.

The other method of giving plants some extra humidity is to buy yourself a hand or pressure sprayer. Use this to give your plants a fine misting of water. The snag with this method is that you'll have to do it fairly frequently as the effect doesn't last very long. Finally, don't spray if the plants are in direct sunlight because the leaves will scorch.

It's also a good idea to keep plants away from sources of indoor heat. If you have to put them on a shelf above a radiator, try and arrange a gap an inch or so wide between shelf and wall, to allow the hot, dry air to flow straight upward.

Above: If you suspect that a plant is pot-bound, tap it out of its pot by placing the stem between your fingers, turning the pot upside down, and giving it a sharp tap on a hard surface. You may need to loosen the root ball first with a knife.
Right: This spider plant certainly needs repotting. The thick roots are spiraled around the base of the pot forming a solid mass.

If you want to take the guesswork out of measuring humidity you can get a hygrometer. This will have a scale of "percent relative humidity" from 0 to 100—at 100 the air is saturated with moisture. For most plants, a relative humidity of around 70 percent is necessary. Below 50 percent is like a desert to a house plant.

There are several prepackaged soil mixes suitable for growing pot plants and these can be bought in most garden shops. Yes, you *could* use garden soil but it's better not to. It varies greatly in content and may contain pests and diseases, so avoid possible disappointment and buy your potting mixes ready sterilized and germ-free.

You can make your own general-purpose potting mix by buying all the ingredients and using the following recipe: two parts good fibrous loam (which you can make from turfs stacked grass downward until they've rotted), two parts rotted leaf mold or garden peat, 1 part *coarse* sand or perlite. If you can't get any leaf mold and use peat instead, add a little bone meal—about a small handful to a bucket of peat.

When you've had your plants for a year or two, or even earlier if you bought any nearly full grown, you may find that some have grown so many roots that they've become "pot-bound" and need repotting. Or you may just want to give them an added plus by way of a soil change. If you can see roots growing through the hole at the bottom of the pot, it's a fairly good sign that the plant is pot-bound—but not always. It may just be that the plant has been grown on a layer of moist sand in the nursery, which encourages roots to grow out. To make sure, gently knock the whole plant from its pot, taking care not to damage any of the leaves, stems, or roots. To do this, place your hand across the top of the pot with the stem between your fingers, turn the pot upside-down and knock the rim against a table or other solid object. It should then slide off the ball of soil. You'll quickly learn the

Left: Put some potting mix in a slightly larger pot, set the roots upon this, and fill in around the sides to within half an inch of the rim top.
Above: Pack the soil firmly with your fingers.

knack. Very occasionally the roots will wedge themselves firmly in the pot. In that case slide a flat-bladed knife between root ball and pot and gently ease the roots away from the pot edge.

If the roots are a thickly tangled mass, or are tightly wound around the base of the pot, then it's time to repot. This is quite a simple operation. Select a pot that is a little bigger than the one the plant came from. This allows the roots to expand and the whole plant to grow, but don't make it too large or the roots won't be able to take up all the water from the extra soil. The excess water will quite likely rot the roots. If the pot you select is a clay pot, cover the drainage hole with a pot shard or some pebbles. Remove the old drainage pebbles, if there were any, from the root ball, and, if the roots are really matted, try to unpick some of them a bit. Don't worry if you break one or two, but it is important not to cause extensive damage to the roots. Put some potting mix at the bottom of the new pot, place the plant in the center

Above: Use potting mix that is on the dry side when repotting, to avoid the mix sticking to your hands. But remember to water the plant afterward.

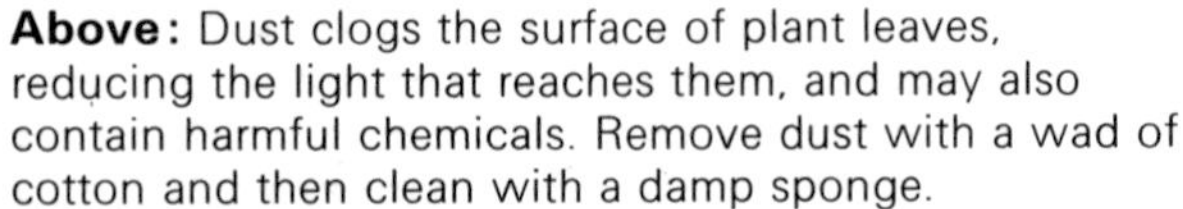

Above: Dust clogs the surface of plant leaves, reducing the light that reaches them, and may also contain harmful chemicals. Remove dust with a wad of cotton and then clean with a damp sponge.

Above: To get a long-lasting protective shine on your plant leaves, use one of the commercial leaf-polishing materials available. The leaves must be clean before the polish is applied—to the upper surface only.

and gradually fill up the sides with more potting mix, pressing it in firmly. Leave at least half an inch between the top of the soil and the top of the pot. Finally, give the newly potted plant a thorough watering.

You may, of course, have a plant that is too big to be easily repotted into a larger pot. In that case you can replace some of the soil by top-dressing. Scrape away the top inch or two of soil and replace it with a fresh lot of potting mix with added nutrients. In just a few days you will notice the difference as your plant begins to look much healthier and revitalized.

Even if your plants don't need repotting, most of them quickly use up the supply of life-giving minerals that were in the potting mix in which they were originally planted. To keep your plants healthy and going strong you must replace these vital minerals from time to time by applying some form of fertilizer.

There are various feed mixtures available to the house-plant gardener, either as liquid, powder, granules, or slow-release tablet and capsule forms.

The most popular way of giving nutrients to house plants is to use a liquid feed—just add a few drops to the water according to the instructions on the bottle and you'll take care of watering and feeding at the same time. The slow-dissolving tablet and capsule fertilizers are buried near the roots and dissolve a little at each watering.

However spotlessly clean your home may be, your house plants will almost certainly collect dust. This not only spoils their appearance, but it clogs the breathing pores, forms a barrier that cuts off light, and often contains harmful chemicals. You'd be wise, therefore, to remove it regularly.

The best way to go about cleaning smooth, shiny-leaved plants is to carefully wipe off as much as you can with a soft dry cloth and then shine up a bit with a wet sponge. Another way is, after first dusting, to put your plants in the bathtub or sink and carefully shower them clean. Even after you have cleaned them, the leaves still tend to be a bit on the dull side—they never seem to keep the gloss they had when new. Don't inflict milk or olive oil on your plants. Instead of polishing the leaves, they only attract more dust. Look around your garden shop for a good leaf polish, usually a branded, water-based wax emulsion, which you wipe on predusted leaves with cotton. It gives them a gorgeous, long-lasting shine.

Whatever you do don't ever spray, cloth-dust, or shine cacti, succulents, hairy-leaved plants such as African violets, or those with a natural leaf bloom (like that on a plum). Instead, dust them with a small soft brush. The kind of brush with a combined rubber bulb used by camera enthusiasts is ideal.

As plants grow, the old leaves and stems wither and look unsightly, and these should be taken off. Often leaves will fall naturally; but if not, cut them off with sharp scissors—don't pull them or you may damage the plant. A bushy plant that gets crowded and tangly will need some of the stems cut out. The bits you've removed can sometimes be used as cuttings.

Many plants have a tendency to get "leggy," and will grow long ungainly stems if they're not treated regularly. With a small bushy plant like, say, the silver-flecked aluminum plant (*Pilea cadierei*), the best way to keep it neat is to pinch out the shoots at the ends of the branches—the young growing parts. It seems a shame to pinch out the hopeful new leaves (or sometimes clip them with scissors), but this does mean that you'll get a couple of new side shoots rather than a single one at the tip of the

Right: Plants with hairy leaves, such as African violets, should not be cleaned with a cloth, nor with water, which will damage them and may cause them to begin rotting. Instead, use a fine soft brush.

Far right: One of the most reliable methods of keeping your plants evenly watered while you are away on vacation is to use the special felt matting shown here. Trail one end of the mat into a partly filled kitchen sink and spread out the remainder on the drainboard. Plants placed on the mat will receive a plentiful supply of water by capillary action. Use plastic pots so that the soil is in close contact with the mat.

Below: If you only have a few plants to keep moist, water them well and place each plant, pot and all, in a large clear plastic bag. Push stakes into the soil to keep the bag clear of the leaves, and tie securely at the top.

branch, and because they grow sideways rather than extending the branch, the shape of your plant is improved.

Really leggy plants, though, must be treated ruthlessly, cutting way back. They'll look like skeletons when you've finished but as long as they are healthy they will soon sprout and form a new neat bush. The long shoots you remove during such drastic pruning can make good cuttings, which we'll be discussing on pages 122–129.

Many of your house plants can benefit from being put outside for a time during the summer. The extra light and air will be like a vacation for them, but do remember to put them in a sheltered position out of scorching midday sun or drying wind, and do check that the soil does not dry out completely. A regular fine misting on warm evenings will help them too.

Generally, only the larger plants with fairly tough leaves can benefit from this treatment. Small, flimsy plants will get damaged by wind and some will be scorched by quite light sun. In any case, do inspect the plants regularly. Remember they could be attacked by aphids, chewing insects, and slugs—creatures they were more protected from inside your house.

Talking of vacations raises the problem of what to do with your plants when you go away for any length of time. Although you can board out your cat or dog, there are no such places for plants. A good idea is to organize a plant-tending team in your neighborhood, so that in turn your plants will be well cared for when you go away.

But failing a plant-minding neighbor, there are various preparations you can make that will keep your plants relatively unaffected by your absence.

If you don't have too many plants, soak the soil thoroughly, then stick two or three stakes, taller than the plant, into the soil. Put each plant into a large, clear plastic bag and tie up the top. Your plants should last unattended like that for several weeks. Another way is to put a layer of gravel on a

deep tray, place your well-watered pots on it and then pack peat around them, watering the whole thing thoroughly so that the peat is quite wet.

One of the latest methods is to use special felt matting. Fill the kitchen sink with water, put the matting on the sink drainer, leaving one end well into the water and then stand your thoroughly watered pots on the felt, and that's all there is to it. The felt will absorb water from the sink and transmit it to the base of the pots, which will then absorb moisture as and when needed. The only disadvantage of this system is that it works only if plants are in plastic pots: this is because their bases are much thinner than those of clay pots, which allows contact between the compost and the matting.

For those of your plants that love very moist soil, you could place them in the bathtub, letting them stand in an inch or two of water, but never for more than eight days or so. After such a spell they should be allowed to drain completely.

Remember not to leave pots on windowsills—move them to the center of a room. They need to be fairly shady and cool to stay moist while you're away.

If you find that some of your plants have wilted when you return, give them immediate first-aid treatment in the form of a generous spraying of water. Then soak the pots. If any plants are beyond rescuing try taking cuttings for propagation.

A Home with Plants in Mind

Only close to the window do plants receive full light on one side (i.e., 50% of available light). The lines on this drawing indicate roughly the zones of light intensity to be found in an average living room.

To have lovely plants growing really well at home is every indoor gardener's ambition. And you're well on the way to success if you keep in mind exactly where you want a plant to grow in your home *before* you make your purchase.

One of the most important considerations to take into account before choosing house plants is the amount of light available in those places you want to grow them. The human eye is very deceptive when deciding how much light is available in a room, because it quickly adjusts to lower light. We can see that the window is bright and other parts of the room are shady, but we don't appreciate just how dark other areas of the room are in relation to most plants' needs. Even by the window, a plant receives only *half* the total light available outside: nearly full light on the window side and no light on the room side.

The direction the light comes from is important, also. If a window facing south gets scorching sun for several hours during the day, few indoor plants would remain unscathed. Even succulents and cacti, used to long periods of sunlight in the desert, are sometimes scorched behind window glass, which intensifies sunlight.

In winter, the difference between night and midday temperature is of tremendous variation at a south-facing window. A west-facing window has similar problems—not quite so serious, perhaps, but in hot weather the late afternoon sun is almost as strong as at midday.

A north-facing window is the best aspect for indoor plants—as long as there are no buildings or trees cutting down the amount of light. You certainly shouldn't be troubled with sun scorch or pots drying out rapidly from the sun's heat. An eastern aspect is almost as good as a northern one, although you must not underestimate the strength of the morning sun in some areas.

If you do have a very sunny window then choose those plants that will tolerate hot sun,

or arrange them so that the sun does not reach them for too long. You can avoid using the windowsill itself and have plants on stands or tables a bit farther from the window. Most indoor plants thrive better in good, unshaded daylight rather than direct sun. Quite a number of plants will stand varying degrees of shade, some right down to five percent of the light outside—ferns, for instance, seem to flourish in the shadiest corners of woods, and many tropical plants, such as the nerve or mosaic plants (fittonias), grow on the jungle floor in very dense shade. But in poor light the "average" plant will get weak and spindly, and produce smaller leaves than normal.

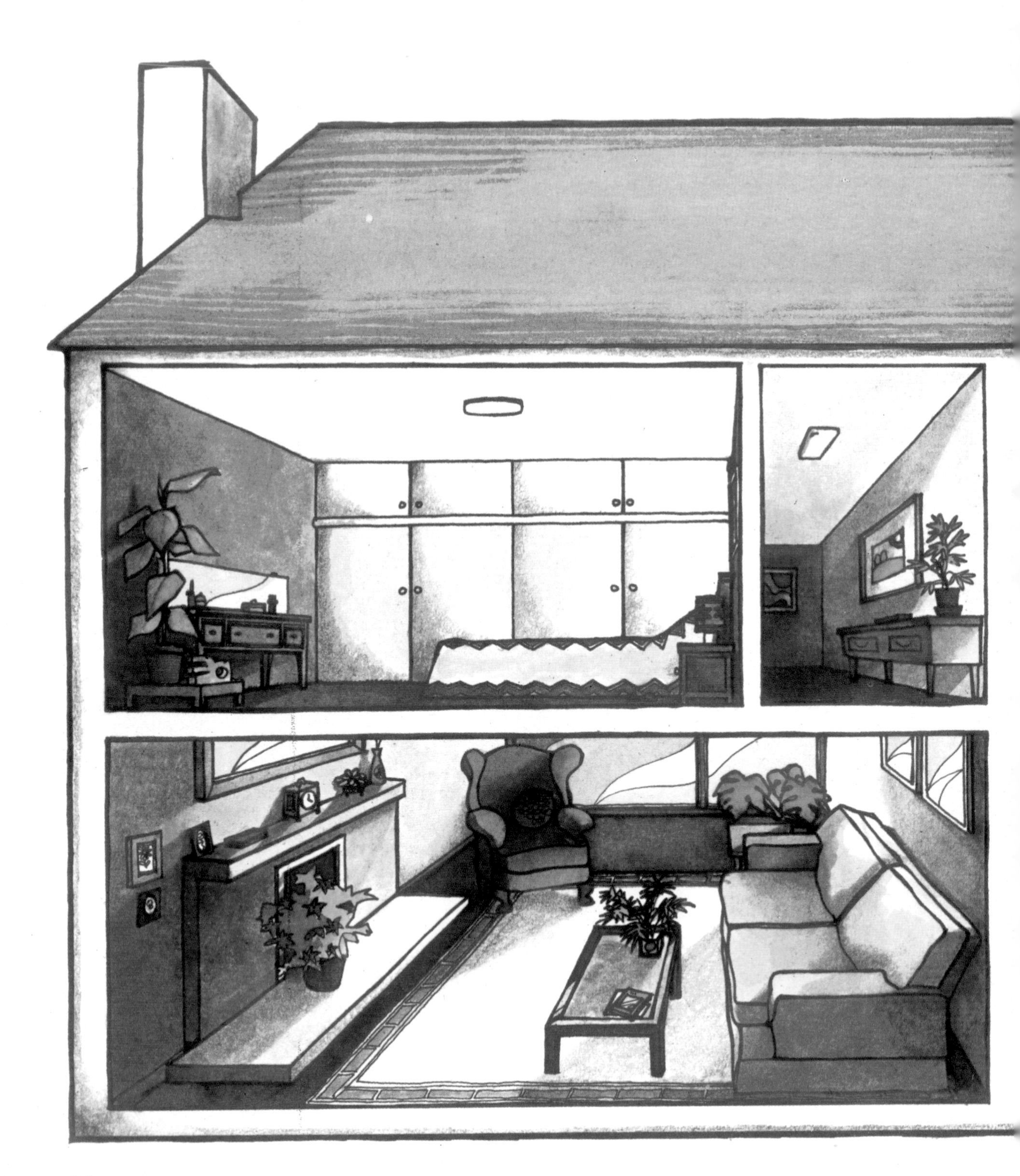

Every house has a number of rooms set aside for a particular purpose, each with its own particular temperature, air humidity, and light. The house on the left illustrates a set of these basic rooms: a living room (below left), with a north-facing window in the farthest wall; a kitchen (below center) with a wide, shallow window; a bedroom (top left), with a south-facing window in the wall that has been cut away; a bathroom (top right) with a small, north-facing window; a hall (top center), with a small window. There may also be other areas, perhaps windowless; staircases, and sometimes (as illustrated below) a small sun room.

In the next section we describe the kinds of plants you can grow in the basic rooms of an average home with some central heating and, in warmer regions, air conditioning. If you do have air conditioning, remember that it dehydrates the atmosphere. It's a good idea to install humidifiers in rooms where plants are to live.

Finally, we should emphasize that plants are fairly tolerant. Although we may say that ideally a particular plant is suitable for a cool bedroom, this doesn't mean that you could not find other places in your home where it would be equally happy.

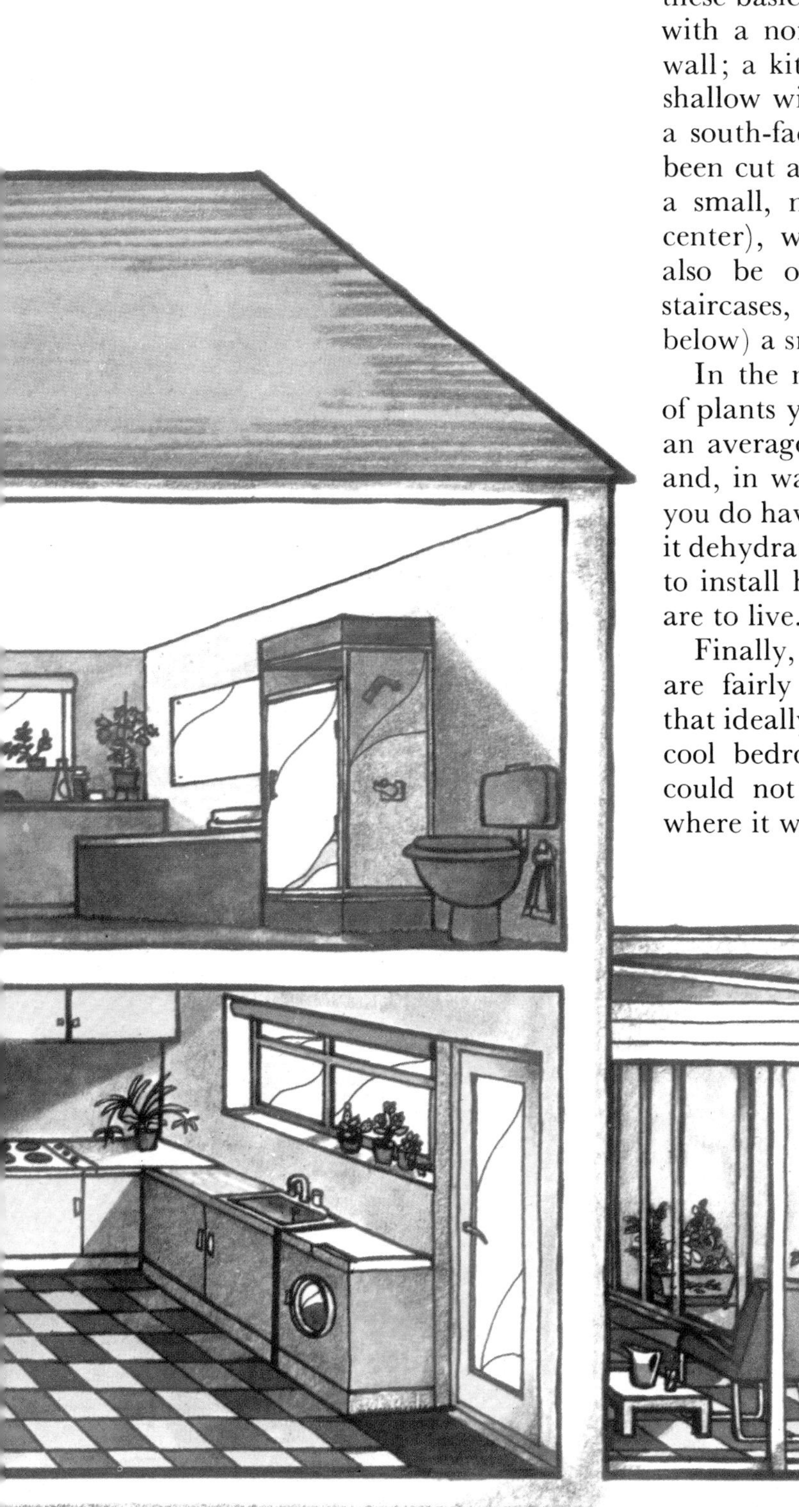

Living Room

Generally heated to around 68°–72°F in winter and lower in summer, perhaps cooler at night. Air probably on the dry side, so give plants local humidity and site them away from radiators.

Left to right: *Cordyline, Schefflera, Dieffenbachia, Dracaena*

LOW OR BUSHY PLANTS	
Anthurium andreanum, A. scherzerianum Flamingo flower	Large, clump-forming plants with attractive leaves and red, pink, or white flowers. Use only lime-free water.
Aphelandra squarrosa "Louisae" Tiger plant, zebra plant	Erect plant with bold, white-veined leaves and yellow flower "cockade." Sensitive to dry air.
Beloperone guttata Shrimp plant	A small-leaved bush with white flowers in pinkish shrimplike bracts. Give good light, water well, keep cool in winter.
Chlorophytum comosum Spider plant	Rosettes of cream-striped, arching leaves produce long stems on which "babies" develop. Very easy in good light.
Crossandra infundibuliformis	Flat-faced, reddish blooms borne for several months. Keep over 70°F in humid conditions.
Impatiens Patient Lucy	Almost continuous production of flowers. Give good light but not sun, and plenty of water.
Maranta Prayer plant, rabbit tracks	Low growing. Give constant temperature, good humidity, indirect light. Related calatheas require high humidity and bright light for good leaf color.
Philodendron (non-climbing)	Big leaves usually deeply cut into "fingers." Generally easy to grow, good in shady corners.
Setcreasea purpurea, Tradescantia, and *Zebrina pendula*	Trailing plants with purple, green, or variegated leaves. Keep moist, well lit, renew often from cuttings.
Spathiphyllum White flag	Like miniature calla lily. Prefers semishade and needs resting October–January.

Anthurium scherzerianum

Aphelandra squarrosa "Louisae"

The living room is a general-purpose room in which people come and go; it's a place for getting together, watching television, smoking, having parties—in fact, it has to be a room where people are more important than plants. This doesn't stop you growing quite a lot of attractive plants, though. The living room is an excellent place for plants arranged as set pieces, either in the form of large single specimens or attractive groupings. However you arrange your plants they should be bold enough to be noticed by your visitors, but tucked safely out of the way of the traffic.

It is the room for the "anywhere plants," including the spider plant (chlorophytum), the ever-flowering patient lucy (impatiens), and the wandering jews—the great tribe of tradescantias and zebrinas ready to form a cascade of foliage almost anywhere. All of

Impatiens

Beloperone guttata

Chlorophytum comosum variegatum

them can stand rough treatment or grow in a way that enables you to keep renewing them.

In the table on page 26 we've listed mainly the low, bushy plants. The taller, erect ones and a number of climbers are dealt with a little later. Form groups from the lower-growing ones, or line them up along window-sills or mantels. In each of the lists are plants with a wide variety of light needs. If you've a really bright window, bring in some cacti and succulents that will accept the sunlight happily. Some of the tougher ferns will grow in the shadier corners. You could bring in some of the plants described later as suitable for corridors and landings, which if anything are even tougher than the "anywheres." And don't forget the great, colorful bromeliad family. Most bromeliads are perfectly happy in the rather indifferent growing conditions likely to be found in a much-used living room.

Top to bottom: *Dracaena deremensis* "Warneckei," *Nephrolepis, Zebrina, Asparagus spr*

Setcreasea purpurea

Tradescantia albiflora "Quicksilver"

Calathea makoyana

Maranta leuconeura "Erythrophylla"

Calathea zebrina

Zebrina pendula

Spathiphyllum wallisii

Dracaena fragrans "Massangeana"

LARGE UPRIGHT PLANTS	
Begonia (stem-forming and shrubby kinds)	Erect plants with handsome foliage. Red, pink, or white flowers. Water freely, but keep well-drained. Provide moist air in part-shade.
Brassaia, or *Schefflera*, *actinophylla* Umbrella plant	Handsome glossy leaves on individual stalks ray out like umbrella ribs from stiff main stem; grows large eventually. Let soil dry out between watering. Average temperatures.
Coffea arabica Coffee tree	Glossy leaves and small, starry, fragrant flowers followed by red or black berries. Likes good light, not hot sun.
Cordyline and *Dracaena*	A large group of tall-growing woody-stemmed plants with long leaves, from very narrow to broad, in assorted colors and stripes. All grow quite easily in average house conditions with good light, not sun.
Dieffenbachia Mother-in-law plant	Dark to pale green leaves with white or cream markings. Give filtered light. Rest with less water in winter.
Ficus Ornamental figs	A large group of trees with stout erect stems. *F. benjamina*, Chinese banyan, has graceful small leaves on hanging branches. *F. diversifolia*, mistletoe fig, needs more water than other varieties. *F. elastica*, rubber plant, has many variegated forms. *F. lyrata*, fiddleleaf fig, grows large. Give good indirect light, let soil become fairly dry between watering. Cool winter rest.
Heptapleurum arboricola Parasol plant	An erect, thin-stemmed, fast-growing shrub bearing dark green glossy leaves on long stalks, composed of narrow radiating leaflets. Resembles *Brassaia* (above) but has lighter effect. Give good light but not hot sun.
Palms	The neatest indoor palm is *Chamaedorea elegans (Neanthe bella). Cocos weddeliana*, a coconut relation, is very slow growing. Larger palms include *Howea* and the pygmy date palm *Phoenix.* Most are easy to grow in good light, but dry air causes leaf withering. Keep soil moist.
Pandanus Screw pine	Palmlike with long, narrow-toothed leaves, often striped. Old plants develop stiltlike roots. Easy to grow but need winter warmth. Let soil dry out between soakings.
Podocarpus macrophyllus Japanese yew	A tall plant with crowded narrow willow-like leaves. Slow-growing so a good-sized specimen will not out-grow its position quickly. Tolerant of a wide range of conditions including quite low winter temperature.

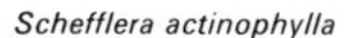

Schefflera actinophylla

Cordyline terminalis

Dieffenbachia amoena with *Nephrolepis*

Chamaedorea elegans in a grouping

Ficus diversifolia

Ficus elastica "Decora"

The large, erect-growing plants suggested in the list on page 30 are best used as single specimens standing alone in large containers to create a focal point. Unless you have a really large room, don't go in for more than one or two really big plants.

Smaller specimens of these erect plants can, of course, go into mixed groupings and there may well be the opportunity to put a number of medium-sized specimens together in one corner, creating a "cool glade" effect.

In time, many of these plants become very tall. This can happen with the ficus, cordylines and dracaenas, and the umbrella plant (brassaia or schefflera); whereas the screw pines (pandanus) grow outward. The question is what do you do when a long-established rubber plant is about to hit the ceiling? You'll just have to behead them! New shoots usually form quite near the point of cut, so keep it fairly low. If the lower stem of a plant is bare of leaves, a cut made well down the stem may encourage new growth to sprout from the base. If you don't want to throw away the part you've cut off, treat it as a cutting and propagate a new plant.

Monstera deliciosa, detail of leaf

CLIMBING PLANTS

Cissus antarctica Kangaroo treebine	Medium-sized, toothed, pale green leaves on quick-climbing stems with tendrils. Easy to grow, but must be out of direct sun. Peaty soil mixes and water persisting in drip tray cause dry brown blotches on leaves. Water only when soil dries out.
Cissus rhombifolia (Also known as *Rhoicissus rhomboidea.*) Grape ivy	A fast climber with small, notched, dark green leaves, growing in threes, reddish underneath in some forms. Treat like *Cissus antarctica*
Monstera deliciosa Split-leaf philodendron	Large, roundish leaves with holes and cuts grow on massive stem with long aerial roots. Give a large pot and feed well or leaves will grow small and uncut. Prefers shade.
Philodendron scandens Sweetheart vine	The easiest of numerous climbing kinds, with small heart-shaped leaves. Can also be allowed to trail. Give a shady spot, avoid hot dry air. Water well, but avoid making soil soggy.
Scindapsus aureus (Also known as *Rhaphidophora aurea.*) Devil's ivy	Yellow markings on heart-shaped leaves, Marble Queen is almost entirely cream-colored. Treat like *Philodendron*.
Syngonium Arrowhead plant	Related to philodendron, and needing same care. Leaves have three or more lobes.

Among climbing house plants are two "any-wheres" suitable for the living room—kangaroo treebine (*Cissus antarçtica*), and grape ivy (*Cissus rhombifolia*). *Philodendron scandens,* although less easy to grow than kangaroo treebine and grape ivy, is more popular.

If you decide on either of the cissus, or the philodendron, you want to be able to move the pots or grow them in one place on permanent supports. Whichever you decide, it's important to remember that these plants grow fast, and if not supported they soon look untidy.

In the right place climbers can be very effective. Train them on fixed string or wire trellis either side of the main living-room window or use them as room dividers, particularly in an "open-plan" home.

In cooler rooms you can add any of the great variety of ivies to your selection of climbers. These look effective when allowed to trail from a height.

Although it's really a climber, there isn't usually enough room indoors for the split-leaf philodendron (monstera). Try growing it in a corner supported by a thick stick or two, more as an unusual green accent than as a screening climber.

Monstera deliciosa

Cissus rhombifolia

Cissus antarctica

Scindapsus aureus

Philodendron scandens

Philodendron erubescens

Cooler Rooms
Bedrooms & Dining Room

Fairly cool, probably between 58°–65°F, higher (68°–70°) for short periods, with adequate air humidity and light from windows.

Araucaria excelsa

Araucaria excelsa Norfolk Island pine	A monkey-puzzle relation with feathery, pale green branches arranged in symmetrical tiers. Almost hardy, so keep it cool. A good specimen plant for a light place.
Ardisia crenata Coral berry	Neat upright evergreen carrying flowers and fruit together, the red berries lasting many months. Give good light, some sun, and water well. Avoid hot dry air.
Asparagus plumosus, A. sprengeri Asparagus fern	Not ferns at all but lilies! They make graceful pendulous plants, or can be trained on supports. Need good indirect light—or leaves will yellow. Soil should be kept moist. Easy to grow, but dislike dry air.
Asparagus meyersii Plume or foxtail asparagus	Forms upright tapering branches of close foliage like miniature cypresses. Easy to grow.
Fatsia japonica Japanese aralia	Big, handsome, hand-shaped glossy leaves. Keep below 70°F. Give good indirect light and keep fairly moist.
Ficus pumila Creeping fig	Small, heart-shaped leaves; climbs or trails. Very hardy, keep as cool as possible.
Grevillea robusta Silk oak	Stiff, ferny leaves on woody, upright stems. Attractive coloring from green-gold to deep green. Tough, prefers temperatures between 50–65°F. Place in partial shade.
Carex morrowii	A grass-like plant, actually a kind of sedge, with long, very narrow arching leaves with a central yellow or white stripe. Sun or shade suit it and it stands cold. Keep moist but not soaking wet.
Hedera Ivy	Many kinds of ivy. A vast range here for the decorator, from tiny leaves to large ones, with white, silvery, cream, and gold patternings or shades. Grow them hanging down, climbing up, or on a frame. Prefer cool, even temperatures and partly shady places.

Fatsia japonica

Table setting with *Ficus pumila, Syngonium, Pilea cadierei,* ivies

Ficus pumila

A few well-chosen plants will add considerably to the attractions of your bedroom decor and are a pleasure to look at when you wake up each morning. Try placing a small plant or two on the dressing table, or the bedside tables. A well-flowering African violet or other flowering pot plant seems particularly suited to a bedroom situation, where they don't have to compete with too many other plants. There may be room for a single large plant like an African linden or Norfolk Island pine in a light corner.

Hanging plants, such as the two kinds of asparagus fern, can flow down over the side of a chest of drawers or from the top of wardrobe closets. There is probably scope, too, for various ivies in similar positions.

Besides the plants mentioned in the list on page 34, many true ferns do well in the

Asparagus plumosus

Philodendron bipinnatifidum and *Begonia rex*

Oplismenus hirtellus variegatus Basket grass	A trailing, short-jointed grass looking much like a tradescantia, with lance-shaped, white variegated, often pink-tinged leaves. Likes very good light. Feed sparingly, and give little water in winter.
Plectranthus oertendahlii Swedish ivy	Looks, and smells, like a hanging or creeping white-variegated mint. Grows fast, likes good indirect light.
Saxifraga stolonifera Strawberry geranium, strawberry begonia	Choose the gold-variegated form of this smallish, clumpy plant with long, threadlike runners carrying babies. Needs good indirect light, never sun. Water well and keep temperatures cool.
Senecio macroglossus variegatum Wax vine	This is a tease plant because it looks so like an ivy with fleshy triangular yellow-patterned leaves. It's really a climber needing some support, but it can trail. Stands hot dry conditions.
Sparmannia africana African linden, house lime	Large, pale green hairy leaves on a many-stemmed shrub. Prune well to prevent it growing too tall. Likes some sun, generous watering and plant food. Can be kept in a smallish pot.

fairly cool conditions. In older houses there may be a fireplace, and here a group of elegant ferns, or even an aspidistra, can look very handsome placed in the old grate.

The cooler rooms in your house are very useful for giving plants a summer rest. The airy conditions will help them recover from their winter stresses of coping with hot, dry rooms—assuming you haven't got a shady garden corner to put your resting plants in. Here, of course, a spare bedroom comes into its own, as long as there's enough light, and you can pack plants out of the way on large plastic trays—but don't let it be a case of out of sight, out of mind. They'll need plenty of water, and possibly pest control.

If you keep your dining room on the cool side, the plants recommended for the bedroom should thrive quite happily there, too. Dining rooms are often suitable for a few large plants or medium-sized groups, and are excellent places to display a collection of antique kitchen utensils like copper saucepans, molds, and fish steamers. They make charming pot holders for groups of plants. Accent your group by adding a flowering plant just before your guests arrive.

On the dining table itself a few unusual plants make a good talking point. Choose low, compact plants in smallish groups.

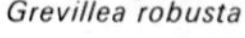

Grevillea robusta

Sparmannia africana in flower

Hedera colchica "Variegata"

Hedera helix "Glacier"

Left to right: *Scindapsus aureus, Ficus elastica, Pellaea rotundifolia*

Kitchen

The kitchen's great bonus for plants is the often steamy atmosphere. Fairly tender, sometimes even difficult plants, should flourish here. All those listed *must* have high humidity.

Episcia Peacock plant, flame violet	Several kinds of spreading or hanging plants related to African violets. Water well and keep out of sun.
Fittonia verschaffeltii Mosaic plant, nerve plant	Spreading plants with silver or red veining on oval leaves. Likes bright, filtered light and plenty of water.
Gynura aurantiaca Velvet plant	Violet-purple hairs on the stems and leaves produce a halo of changing color on this semi-climber according to the direction you look at it. Needs maximum light, plenty of water and misting, and regular cutting back. Nip out flower buds, they have an unpleasant smell.
Helxine soleirolii *(Soleirolia soleirolii)* Angel's tears, baby's tears	Tiny round leaves form dense creeping or hanging mats. Silver and gold forms exist. Keep moist and away from sun.
Hypocyrta nummularia Goldfish plant	Yellow flowers on hanging stems resemble goldfish. Partial shade is best with high humidity. Keep soil moist.
Peperomia	A wide range of small plants with variously shaped and colored leaves. Some varieties make clumps, others are trailers. Give good filtered light. Don't overwater.
Pilea	A range of bushy or wide-spreading plants with oval leaves in intriguing patterns and textures. Prefer slight shade. Silver-marked *P. cadierei*, aluminum plant, should be cut back regularly to encourage bushiness. Keep soil moist but well drained.
Selaginella Moss fern, spike moss	Little plants that make attractive bushlets, sometimes variegated. *S. apoda* is almost hardy but others need heat. Keep shady and never let dry out.

A variety of plants including an African violet enlivens a large kitchen.

Episcia cupreata

Gynura aurantiaca

What better place than the kitchen—often the most lived in, certainly the most worked in room in the house—for a display of plants to balance the pots and pans, cupboards, stove and all the rest of the equipment.

A cupboard or a shelf may often provide a surface for a plant. Make it an upright one for a cupboard, though—a trailer will probably get in the way of the door. Perhaps there's room for an erect, neat-growing specimen in a corner somewhere. The best place for plants, however, is likely to be the windowsill. A kitchen windowsill, unless exposed to scorching sun, may be ideal for rather delicate plants if the conditions are

Peperomia magnoliaefolia "Variegata" (left) and *P. caperata*

Pilea cadierei

Pilea mollis "Moon Valley"

right—fairly warm and plenty of moisture. There, under your eye, the special plants are certain to receive the attention they need.

Of course, if your windowsill doesn't have such ideal conditions, there are any number of hardier, small bushy plants that will live there, instead, especially the marantas and the smaller bromeliads. African violets seem to be great favorites for kitchen windowsills on the north or east side of the house or apartment. If it's very sunny, this is an ideal place for succulents and cacti (but watch for spines if your hands are likely to brush past the plants as you work).

Treat yourself to an occasional flowering pot plant that will either brighten your daily chores or add inspiration to your culinary creations—depending on your view of cooking. As the days pass you can see the buds opening and the flowers developing. When the flowers have faded, buy another plant.

Many people find space for a small bay tree in the kitchen, but it's difficult to grow other herbs there successfully. Mostly they demand more sunlight than even a bright window is likely to give, and become thin and spindly all too soon. However, your kitchen is a good place for many of the seeds and sprouts mentioned in the section "Plants from Leftovers" on pages 112–121.

Bathroom

Plants for bathrooms and kitchens can usually be interchanged, for the bathroom also has moisture released into the air two or three times a day.

Aglaonema "Silver Queen"

Acorus gramineus Grass-leaved flag	A hardy miniature sweet flag making foot-high clumps of narrow erect leaves striped with yellow or white. Prefers good light and can stand in a saucer of water.
Aglaonema Chinese evergreens	Erect plants with long, narrow, pointed leaves, beautifully colored and marbled—rather like miniature dieffenbachias (to which they are related). Use soft water and try not to move the plants around.
Cyperus Umbrella plants	Miniatures of the papyrus rush, with green umbrella flower heads. The slender *C. alternifolius* likes its roots literally in water but others do not want so much moisture. Like good light.
Dizygotheca elegantissima False aralia, thread leaf	Narrow, notched leaflets radiate from a central point on erect stems, making a very airy effect. Don't let soil get wet or cold, apply fertilizer regularly and keep out of the sun.
Hypoestes sanguinolenta Pink polka-dot plant, freckle face	Small, oval, pointed leaves are speckled with pink and purple. Can grow leggy so need regular pruning. Keep warm and just moist.
Pellionia	Small-leaved trailing or creeping plants with dark markings. Like bright light but avoid direct sun. Plenty of water and high humidity.
Pittosporum	Nearly hardy shrubs of graceful open habit. If your bathroom is big enough try a specimen plant—one of the best is *P. undulatum variegatum*—Victorian box—with oblong, wavy-edged leaves edged pale yellow.
Rhoeo spathacea (or *discolor*) Moses-in-the-cradle	An unexpected relation of tradescantias with a rosette of soft, narrow, pointed leaves, purple underneath, sometimes variegated, and flowers in curious boat-shaped containers. Prefers half-shade, but adapts readily to adverse conditions.

A crested form of *Pteris* fern sets off this modern bathroom.

Cyperus alternifolius (grown in pebbles)

The generally moist air found in bathrooms often makes them perfect places for rather difficult plants. In the moist air plants such as African violets can be grouped, as long as there is a fairly deep windowsill with plenty of light. If the light isn't too good, ferns of all kinds will usually succeed.

The dedicated plant lover will be tempted to turn the bathroom into a jungle of greenery. Most of the general-purpose plants suggested for the living room will grow here—clumpy ones, tall specimens, and climbers alike. In smaller bathrooms it may be better to keep to just three or four good specimens.

The bathroom is one place where plain green—particularly the delicate, cool green found in most ferns—comes off especially well with a white or plain-colored decor. Foliage always looks good against tiles.

One important point—do keep to soft-foliage plants! While most plants are harmless if brushed against, especially ferns and asparagus ferns, it isn't pleasant to get stuck on a cactus or pricked by a sharp bromeliad leaf when rubbing yourself dry.

Above: Ferns suit the average bathroom well, enjoying the high humidity and tolerating the lack of light. The *Pteris* ferns on the shelves and *Asplenium nidus* by the sink are in neat containers that complement the glass and tile decor.

Dizygotheca elegantissima

Bathroom garden, including ferns, asparagus ferns, and *Ficus benjamina*

Hypoestes sanguinolenta

Rheo spathacea

Halls and Landings

Drafts, fluctuating temperatures, dryish air, and a good deal of shade create problems, although landings and staircases often have plenty of light.

Left to right: *Columnea, Oleander (Nerium), Chamaedorea elegans*

Aspidistra elatior Cast-iron plant	So called by Victorians because it could survive gas fumes. Long, pointed leaves, fairly broad, sometimes variegated, make a loose clump. Avoid sun and keep moist but *don't* let the pot stand in water.
Aucuba japonica Spotted laurel	This hardy shrub demands little care and is ideal in a cool position with medium light. Choose one of the varieties with gold flecks on the leaves which light up an otherwise dull plant.
Clivia miniata Kaffir lily	A large, clump-forming plant with long, arching, strap-shaped leaves in two rows and, from December to April, heads of large orange lily flowers. Don't repot old plants often. Water when soil begins to dry out and feed well in summer. Best kept around 55°F in winter.
Fatshedera lizei	A hybrid of ivy and fatsia producing erect stems with large, ivy-shaped leaves. Stands shade better than fatsia, likes lots of water and best kept quite cool in winter. There is an attractive variegated variety.
Liriope muscari Lily-turf	A perfectly hardy plant which will however stand temperatures up to 60–65°F and will tolerate semi-shade. It has long narrow strap-shaped leaves, striped yellow in the variegated form, and may produce blue flower spikes in late summer.
Sansevieria trifasciata "Laurentii" Snakeplant	An unusual-shaped plant with sword-like, wavy, vertical leaves, normally yellow-banded, but can revert to plain mottled green. Valuable in many rooms for contrast of form. Will stand dry, stuffy air and some shade. Allow to nearly dry out between waterings, then soak.
Tolmiea menziesii Piggy-back plant	A small, clump-forming, bright green plant that produces babies on the older leaves. Prefers filtered light, fresh, cool conditions, and plenty of water. It is quite hardy.

Clivia miniata

Those parts of the house that aren't rooms—the entry hall, halls, landings, staircases—present difficult conditions for most plants.

Nevertheless, these often dull areas can be enlivened with a spot of living greenery. A single handsome plant or grouping in the entry way makes a cheery welcome for visitors, and stairs often provide interesting places where plants can be displayed.

The plants listed on page 46 are those that can stand adverse conditions and a little neglect. But many of the plants already mentioned will usually grow in hallways and other odd spaces, too. You may find you have just the spot for a chlorophytum, or a cissus, or one of the tough ferns such as cyrtomium, or, if the light is good, some of the many bromeliads. Ivies prefer shade as long as the air is not hot and dry.

The important thing is not to forget any plants that you put in hallways when it comes to routine watering and tending. In fact, make a point of keeping an extra special eye on them. As soon as they begin to show signs of distress whisk them away to a better-lighted spot to recuperate—a spare bedroom, for instance—and replace them with something else.

Fatshedera lizei "Variegata"

Tolmiea menziesii

Sansevieria trifasciata "Laurentii"

Aspidistra elatior and variegated form

Sun Room

The light and airiness produce near-greenhouse conditions, and it is easy to create local humidity with pebble trays. Protect plants against scorching sun.

Bougainvillea glabra

Abutilon Flowering maple, Chinese lantern	Large, evergreen shrubs with bell or lantern-shaped flowers in yellow, orange, red, or purplish shades. Pinch out regularly to encourage flower and control growth. Rest at around 55°F in winter.
Allamanda	Plants with sumptuous lemon to gold trumpet-shaped blooms most of the summer. *A. cathartica* is a very vigorous climber, *A. neriifolia* more of a shrub and reasonably compact. They need large pots, plenty of food, and warm humid conditions.
Bougainvillea	Likes subtropical conditions. Indoors can be kept bushy by pruning, or makes long stems to train on walls. Papery flowers typically magenta, also scarlet, pink, or orange. Water well while growing. Keep cool in winter (40°–45°F).
Callistemon citrinus Bottlebrush	A bushy shrub with red flowers in cylindrical spikes looking just like a bottle-cleaning brush. Only needs protection from frost in winter.
Citrus	Most citrus fruits—oranges, lemons, grapefruits—can be grown easily in containers. (*C. mitis*, the Calamondin, has miniature oranges.) Water well. Keep cool in winter.
Datura (several kinds) Angel's trumpets	Shrubs with large, hanging, trumpet flowers, white, yellow, or red, very fragrant. Can be kept bushy by hard February pruning. Give plenty of fresh air and a little shade, watch for red spider mite, and keep cool in winter.
Eucalyptus Gum tree	Young plants of any kind of *Eucalyptus* can be grown in pots, or you can easily raise *E. globulus* from seed—it will reach 8 feet in two years so grow new ones each spring! Lovely for silvery aromatic foliage; very easy apart from enormous thirst on hot days.

Abutilon megapotamicum

Fuchsia Lady's eardrop	Medium sized shrubs that can be trained as bushes or standards or, in some cases, hanging plants, with the familiar pendulous flowers. Give plenty of water. Grow best in half shade. Very cool in winter.
Hibiscus rosa-sinensis Chinese hibiscus	Bushy, evergreen plants with showy flowers in red, pink, gold, or white. Like good light but not full sun. Fertilize every two weeks when in flower, water well. Prefer winter temperature of 55°F.
Hoya Wax flower, wax plant	The climbing hoyas have slender stems, thick, glossy leaves and extraordinary pinkish waxy blooms in small clusters. Like good light. Leave potbound to encourage blooming. Keep almost dry and on the cool side (50°–55°F) in winter.
Jasminum Jasmine	Various kinds are very easy to grow as climbers. Pink-flushed, very fragrant *J. polyanthum* flowers in winter; yellow *J. primulinum* in early spring; white fragrant *J. sambac* in summer. Keep all cool in winter.
Passiflora	Rampant climbers with extraordinary blooms in blue, purple, and various shades of red. Choose hardy *P. caerulea* for cool winter conditions, more exciting *P. quadrangularis* or *P. racemosa* for warmth. Give bright light when in flower.
Pelargonium Geranium	A wide variety of leaf and flower forms. *P. zonale*, has bunched flowers in many colors all summer long. *P. grandiflorum* the regal pelargonium has more exotic, open flowers, often contrastingly blotched, mainly in early summer. *P. peltatum*, ivy geranium, is a trailer with bunched flowers. There are also scented-leaf kinds. All are bushy and easy to grow, mostly liking a cool winter rest; *P. grandiflorum* prefers around 50°F. Give good light and plenty of fresh air.
Plumbago capensis Cape leadwort	A lovely plant carrying pale blue or white starry flowers from spring until fall. Grows as a loose bush and is easily trained against a wall. Give it plenty of space for roots. Cool in winter (45–50°F).
Tibouchina semidecandra Glory bush	An erect shrub with large fattish royal-purple flowers in later summer, and attractive pointed-oval leaves. Needs cutting back in spring to keep it in bounds. Only needs frost protection and little water in winter.

Standard and bush Fuchsias frame pots of regal *Pelargonium* and blue *Plumbago*.

The sun room is often turned into an extra sitting room, or sometimes is used as a kind of halfway room between house and garden. Used as a sitting room, it can take some of the ordinary house plants, and these should grow well.

The near-greenhouse conditions produced in a sun room will give you an opportunity to grow a number of near-exotic plants. So, if you're a really keen plant lover you will be able to use it as a place where you can add to your repertory—turn it into a plant room, in fact.

Although there are many plants suitable for growing in a sun room, not all of them like the same conditions. You must decide whether you want a light, airy room or one that is hot and humid (or hot and dry). Assuming that your sun room will be used by you and your family, we have chosen

Fuchsia Beacon

Citrus mitis

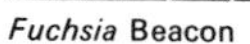

Plumbago capensis

Sun-room display mainly of pelargoniums, with ferns and ivies

Hibiscus rosa-sinensis

Passiflora caerulea

Hoya carnosa

mainly those plants that like light and airy conditions.

There are very few house plants that can tolerate strong sunlight, so if the room has a transparent roof, screen your plants (and yourself) from full scorching sunlight by fitting reed or Venetian blinds. You'll find you will need all the ventilation you can get in hot weather, too.

If your sun room is a real sun trap, then you have the ideal conditions for growing cacti and succulents, and you could make a display of large specimens along the outer walls.

Most of the plants listed like fairly cool conditions in winter; even the more exotic ones need a maximum of only 55° or perhaps 60°F, because they are resting at that time. Generally, sun rooms are, by their very nature, less used in winter so that the winter temperatures recommended are quite easily met. If you keep the place warmer, however, choose some of the orthodox house plants already mentioned that like fairly high winter temperatures.

There's no doubt that, if you try, you can experiment by growing a different and exciting range of plants in a suitable sun room. This is one part of the house where the tropical jungle effect never looks out of place. Other rooms indoors have different purposes, and plants remain subordinate to these. The sun room, however, can be planned largely for plants. Use it just to sit in and enjoy the sun coming through the clustering foliage. Enjoy the fragrances, too, that mingle with the smell of humid growth. Here you can escape from everything and think yourself far away from ordinary life.

Regal pelargonium "Summertime"

Flowering Plants for Accent

A dash of brilliant or subtle color can often accent a plant grouping. And there are lots of very attractive and colorful plants you can buy that will add just that splash of color and life to a flowerless and perhaps slightly dull group of foliage plants. For instance, try teaming up pale pink primroses with your bluish or gray-green foliage plants, or perhaps some gorgeous, deep rust-colored chrysanthemums with plants that have glossy dark green leaves.

Most flowering plants aren't worth the trouble of keeping once they're past their best—unless you're lucky enough to have a greenhouse or plenty of other suitable space. When they've finished flowering, be ruthless and throw them away.

The majority of these temporary flowering plants will look their best only if they're kept fairly cool and away from very bright light. Unfortunately, this means that many won't last long if you like a warm home! As compensation, give them lots of water to make up for what they lose in the heat and dryness—but make it a golden rule never to let them stand in it. They will also benefit from an occasional misting of water.

If the soil does dry out, however, flowers, buds, and leaves will droop and then fall off, so do watch them carefully; you must also make sure that they're not in a draft. All these plants benefit if you feed them with a soluble fertilizer as soon as you buy them—it helps to open the buds—and again three weeks later if they're still going strong.

Around Christmas you will find azaleas in the florist shops and often in supermarkets and variety stores. They come in all sorts of brilliant or soft and delicate colors; in fact, you could say there's at least one to suit each of your moods. When you come to choose one for your home do check that it has lots of buds and that it's been watered properly. The best way to water azaleas is to put the whole pot in water and leave it to soak until the air bubbles stop, then drain away any excess. Very often azaleas are potted in pure peat and may also have had some of their roots chopped off, so make sure they are kept moist and cool.

Pot ericas, or Cape Heaths, small shrubby plants with masses of white, pink, or mauve bell-like flowers, have a similar moisture problem. If they dry out, the small leaves will drop at once.

There are many different kinds of cyclamen that grow in the wild but the one sold as a house plant is *Cyclamen persicum*; once in flower it likes to be kept rather cool and humid, so sink the pot in a tray of peat and keep that nicely moist. Don't get any water on the "crown" (the knobby tuber at the base of the stems) or it will quickly rot. Feed it regularly and twist away any dead leaves or flowers, making sure that you take the whole of the stem. Cyclamen come in red, shades of pink, and white.

From early December until after the New Year you can buy *Solanum capsicastrum*, which goes by two names—Jerusalem cherry or Christmas cherry. This plant has lovely shiny round red berries the size of grapes. Although they look good enough to eat,

Right: The cineraria has daisy-like large or small flowers, and can be bought in a range of gay colors. It is only an annual, however, so when it has finished blooming it should be thrown away.

Above: The Christmas azalea—seen here with a spider plant and a fern—is not hardy like the garden kinds. Even so, it should be kept cool. Keep the peaty soil just moist with lime-free water.

don't—they're poisonous. It is not a plant to have around with small children. Keep your plant very cool and moist if you don't want it to drop all its leaves and fruits at one time. To get it to fruit another year, put it outside in summer, giving it an occasional misting to help the flowers to "set" fruits.

The pepper or chilli plant, *Capsicum annuum*, has attractive little red or yellow pepperlike fruits (they're not poisonous, but they're not generally eaten either). If you let your plant get too dry it'll react the same way as your solanum—its leaves and fruits will fall off. Unlike the cherry, it is an annual and can be discarded when it's finished. Both pepper and cherry are very festive little plants, and go well with Christmas decorations. One last word of caution. If your house is heated with gas, don't bother with either one, for no matter what you do the slightest trace of gas fumes causes their leaves and fruits to drop.

The poinsettia, *Euphorbia pulcherrima*, is of course *the* Christmas plant with its large, bright red leaflike bracts surrounding the insignificant yellow flowers. There are also more subtle varieties with pink, cream, or white bracts. If you like a cool room, look out for the Mikkelsen varieties. They will enjoy temperatures around 55–65°F. Once again, either underwatering or overwatering will make buds and lower leaves drop off. To be sure you're getting it just right, wait until the leaves droop very slightly before watering.

Kalanchoe blossfeldiana will flourish in average to warm rooms, for it is a succulent. It has small red, salmony, coral pink, or sometimes white flowers in clusters at the end of long stems. Kalanchoe is an easy plant; it loves bright sunlight, and needs little water.

In early spring you will find in florist shops the calceolaria, or slipper flower, with spectacular pouch-shaped blooms in a range of glorious "hot" colors—gorgeous sunshine yellow through flaming scarlet, speckled or plain. It seems to be particularly attractive to aphids, so keep a look out for them.

Cineraria, or more correctly *Senecio cruen-*

tus, has daisy-like flowers in a wide variety of colors, some with white centers. Those in shades of blue and purple look particularly handsome. This is another plant prone to aphids, so act quickly at the first signs. Both calceolaria and cineraria must be kept as cool as possible; and both, being annuals, should be discarded after flowering.

There are several different kinds of indoor primroses with either blue, red, pink, or white flowers. The most popular is *Primula obconica*, even though it does give some people a mild skin rash from its leaves; fortunately, it's the only one that does. If you don't want to risk getting a rash, try one of the other primroses, such as *Primula malacoides* or *Primula sinensis*, for they are all pretty. The pot primroses will stand more warmth than cinerarias and calceolarias.

Above: Yellow calceolaria and *Kalanchoe blossfeldiana* make an informal, temporary tabletop group with an ivy whose fronds have been attractively threaded among the blooms.

Left: The poinsettia is a kind of spurge, *Euphorbia pulcherrima*. Its color comes from large floral leaves around small flowers. There are now varieties in red, pink, cream, or white.

Below: The Christmas or Jerusalem cherry, *Solanum capsicastrum*, carries its round fruits for many weeks. This one is set against a background of grevillea and a fern and an ivy.

Left: Dwarf pot chrysanthemums, which can be bought all year around, have been treated with special chemicals to keep them small during their first year of flowering. Plant them in the garden to flower the next year, when they will grow to their natural size of three or four feet.

Below left: Potted hydrangeas need to be kept well-watered and in a cool room, if possible. After flowering, plant outside in a moist, shady place; but don't be surprised if the flowers change color!

Below: *Primula obconica*, the commonest indoor primrose. Handle carefully, as it gives a few people a mild skin rash.

By early spring your local nursery may have potted hydrangeas: white, red, pink, or deep blue. These require lots of water so give them regular, generous helpings. When flowering is over you can put them in the garden in a moist, shady place.

Chrysanthemums are available all year round in lots of superb colors, some rich, some subtle and soft. They also have different-shaped flowers, from small pompons to large flower heads with incurved petals. Some new ones are slender and delicate-looking with very fine florets. These pot chrysanthemums have been dwarfed with special chemicals and if you try growing them another year you'll find they shoot up to three or four feet. They will droop dramatically in their pots if the soil even starts to dry out, so be sure to keep it moist at all times, and cut off any dead flowers at once.

In summer, oddly enough, there are fewer flowering pot plants about. One that you may pick up is the German violet, *Exacum affine*. It grows to only a few inches high and has a mass of small bright mauve flowers, which are delicately fragrant. You should be able to keep it in flower for most of the summer in a shaded place.

The gloxinia is one of the most handsome flowering plants, with large velvety trumpet flowers in many rich colors. It grows from a tuber and produces a rosette of leaves. Really a warm greenhouse plant, it must be given a moist atmosphere or the buds will shrivel. Its relation, achimenes, is more bushy with smaller flowers, and tolerates dry air better; but both will appreciate having the pot placed in a container of moist peat.

The easiest temporary summer plant—the coleus—doesn't flower, or if it does you should cut the spikes off. Its glory is in its multicolored leaves, with varied patterns of bronze, red, purple, pink, green, yellow, and white. The names Flame Nettle or Painted Nettle are well chosen, except that the coleus doesn't sting! Feed it regularly but don't overwater or it will become very limp and may not recover. Pinch out the central growing tips to encourage bushy growth.

Above: The gorgeous gloxinia, with huge velvety trumpet-shaped flowers, must have a really moist, warm spot or the buds simply will not open. It is really a greenhouse plant.

Below: The glory of many kinds of coleus lies in the multicolored leaves, which earn them such names as Flame Nettle or Painted Nettle (though they do not sting!). The tiny flowers should be nipped out.

African Violets

Few flowering house plants can be quite as rewarding as African violets. You'll find these pretty little rosette plants, known botanically as *Saintpaulia ionantha*, available in very many varieties, with colors ranging from varying shades of blue through purple, pink, crimson, bicolored, and white; they may be single or double flowered; the leaves can be dark green or variegated, plain or fringed. The choice is immense.

When you buy saintpaulias, choose dark foliage (unless, of course, they're purposely variegated) and thick flower stems, and whatever colored flowers take your fancy.

As house plants, African violets can be temperamental, but if you're willing to give them just what they need you'll be rewarded with flower-covered plants almost all year.

One of the first things you should get right is the amount of warmth and humidity they like best. The plants like to be kept at a steady 65–70°F, though they will tolerate a slightly lower temperature at night.

Another important point is that if African violets are to flower continuously, they should have at least 14 hours of light a day. On dark or wintry days you can supplement the natural light by using artificial lighting. Don't put them too near ordinary electric light bulbs, though, or they may scorch, just as they will in strong sunlight. The ideal "extra" light is a fluorescent mercury vapor tube, especially the Gro-lux type. Devoted hobbyists and specializers usually have glass cabinets with these tubes built in.

Along with warmth and light your African violets will need an adequately humid atmosphere for them to grow and flower successfully. The easiest way to provide the humidity they need is to place the pot in a container of peat, which you must keep constantly damp. Alternatively, stand the pot on pebbles in a shallow dish of water and add more water as the level goes down. The warmer your room, the more important it is for you to maintain this humidity—which also, by the way, cuts down the need for very frequent watering. Surprisingly, African violets can put up with dry roots—for a time—as long as they're in the right atmosphere. In fact you'd do better to keep the plants a bit on the dry side as overwatering can lead to rotting and eventually to the death of the plant.

It's quite safe to water the plants from the top of the pot, but do make sure that none gets on the leaves, as they can rot fairly quickly. Naturally, from time to time a leaf or flower will die. When that happens, pull it and the stem cleanly away from the rest of the plant. If you don't, any remaining dead material can become rotten and possibly affect the crown of the plant.

When you water, try to use water that is the same temperature as the room the plants are in. You needn't actually take the temperature of the water itself; the simplest way is to let it stand overnight in the room.

Unless you really like to repot, you'll find that African violets score over most other plants on this point. They actually flower best when the roots are fairly crowded in the

Left: Low-growing, rosette-forming African violets, or saintpaulias, can be bought in a wide range of colors and make most rewarding house plants. When they have become acclimatized they will produce flowers for most of the year.

Left: One of the joys of African violets is the ease with which they propagate. All you have to do is cut off outer leaves and push their stems into pots of light compost. Soon you will have new plants.

Left: After six to eight weeks, small leaves appear at the base of the old leaf, which can be cut away and started again.

Left: If young plants form more than one crown, they should be separated to avoid crowding.

Right: Gently pull the individual crowns apart and replant them in separate pots. Use fresh potting compost, as by now they will appreciate more food.

pot. If you think repotting is needed, then moisten the new soil first. This is because you must not water saintpaulias thoroughly after potting as you do other plants. And another important point: only repot between May and August.

The best potting soil for your African violets is a peat-based mix. You can buy special prepackaged African-violet mixes but if you like mixing your own, use 3 parts peat, 1 part light loamy soil, and 1 part coarse sand. You won't need to put shards in the pots with the peat mixtures.

Feed your violets about once a month in summer, using a standard liquid fertilizer, diluted according to instructions. Toward the end of summer use a tomato food—the extra potash will help winter flowering.

The easiest way to increase your African violets is to propagate from leaf cuttings. All you have to do is take a healthy leaf from your favorite plant, put it into a pot of propagating peat mix, keep it moist and warm, and in six to eight weeks there will be a tiny plantlet around the stem of the old leaf. From then on all you do is wait until the plantlet forms roots and increases to a more manageable size, then carefully detach it and put it into its own pot. If you cut the plantlet from the parent leaf carefully, you can use the leaf again—and again! Leaf cuttings work just as well if the parent leaf is put into water instead of soil.

In time the neat rosette of the young African violet splits up and develops into a cluster of crowns. Not only do these look unsightly but they also overcrowd the pot. Then it's time to separate them, which isn't easy with such a brittle plant.

Knock the plant carefully out of its pot and place it on newspaper. Very gently, pull at the separate crowns and try to tease them apart. If they won't part, cut through any leaves and roots in the way with a small sharp knife. Repot each piece in its own pot and they will soon grow into rosettes.

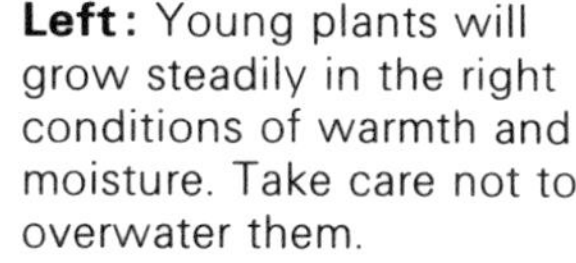

Left: Young plants will grow steadily in the right conditions of warmth and moisture. Take care not to overwater them.

Left: When the leaves begin to overlap the pot, give an occasional weak feed to help the young plant develop buds and build up a strong rosette.

Right: Three to four months after starting from a single leaf, you can expect the new plant to bloom.

Vriesea splendens, sometimes called flaming sword, can be kept as happy indoors (above) as it is in the ideal environment, a hothouse (left). It is a typical epiphytic bromeliad with hard, arching leaves forming a water-retaining "vase" in the center, which must always be kept full of water. The bright red of the flower spike, which lasts for many months, comes from bracts surrounding the small flowers.

Bromeliads: The Tropical Touch

If you want to grow something exciting, decorative, and startlingly beautiful, then bromeliads are for you. In spite of their exotic, jungly appearance they don't have to be grown by experts or in very special conditions. In fact, with a little care, bromeliads can be made to grow in most of our homes.

For the pleasure and interest these fascinating plants will give you, it's worthwhile knowing about them in some detail. To start with, there are two distinct kinds of bromeliad: the *epiphytes*, which grow on trees, and the *terrestrials*, which grow at ground level. The epiphytic bromeliads often grow high up in the branches of jungle trees. Their roots function mainly to keep a grip on their host. Any nourishment they need comes from the air and the rain, absorbed through their leaves. Epiphytic bromeliads sometimes go by the name "air plants" because of their growing habit, and sometimes "vase plants" because the center of each rosette often forms a watertight vase that holds rainwater or dew. The terrestrial bromeliads, on the other hand, grow just like other plants and take their nourishment from the soil. All bromeliads are basically rosette-shaped, with fairly tough leaves that vary in length, thickness, and color in the different kinds of plant. Incidentally, their leaves sometimes have very sharp spines along the edge, so take care where you place the plants about your home!

The ideal temperature for bromeliads is the average home temperature of around 70°F, but they will tolerate even cool rooms, down to, say, 55°F. Best of all they like to be kept at an even temperature and don't mind too much if the air is dry.

You'll find the bromeliads' needs simple enough to satisfy. The most important thing to remember with the vase type is to keep it filled with water, preferably rainwater. Occasionally, change the water (try using a bulb-type roast baster for this) so that it doesn't become stagnant. The roots of all bromeliads should be kept only just moist—overwatered, soggy soil causes the roots to rot and part company with the rest of the plant. Although you should give them plenty of good light, most epiphytic bromeliads don't need sunshine and will grow perfectly well in a warm, partly shaded place.

In their jungle home epiphytic bromeliads get most of their nourishment from the nutrients dissolved in the moist air and from the rain and dew, but in an indoor environment where the air is usually dry (and not, we hope, thick with chemicals released from rotting vegetation!), we can make up for this by giving them some nourishment at the roots, particularly when the plants are young. Terrestrials can be potted, watered, and fed the same as other house plants.

A good potting mixture for bromeliads is made up of one-third pine needles or sphagnum moss, one-third leaf mold, and one-third peat. Alternatively, a peat-based potting soil can be used. Feeding is not so important, but you can give them an occasional very weak dose of liquid fertilizer during the growing season. Keep your bromeliad in as small a pot as possible. Repot only if the plant becomes top-heavy and tends to overbalance.

Each rosette of a plant will flower only once. After flowering and producing a number of offshoots that you can separate and put into pots, the parent plant will gradually die. Leave the young plants

Above: The pineapple is the only fruiting member of the bromeliads. The spectacular variegated forms are the ones most often grown as house plants.

Above: *Neoregelia carolinae* "Tricolor" makes a widespread, flat plant up to two feet across.
Below: One of the earth stars, *Cryptanthus tricolor*. These small plants are good for bottle gardens.

attached to the parent plant for as long as possible. The more mature they are before they're removed, the better chance they have of surviving. Finally, cut them off cleanly with whatever roots of their own they have produced, and place them in individual small pots. You may prefer to leave the youngsters as a cluster. In that case remove the old rosette with a sharp knife when it finally gets unsightly. Keep the young bromeliads warm until they're fully rooted.

There are literally hundreds of bromeliads, both epiphytic and terrestrial, ranging from tiny plants a few inches across to monster-sized ones with two-foot rosettes. Not all these plants have found their way onto the house-plant market yet but there is quite a wide choice. Buy whatever kinds you find—new ones are always being introduced.

The ones you'll see most often for sale include the variegated forms of the pineapple *Ananas comosus*. The bright gold and green forms have varying amounts of pink on the stiff, spiny leaves. They are beautiful plants and eventually grow a little pink pineapple on a stalk from the center.

The pineapples are terrestrial bromeliads and have no vase. Other terrestrials are the cryptanthus, or earth stars, small plants often in attractive browny or silvery tones with various kinds of striping and banding. *Cryptanthus tricolor* is a brilliant mixture of cream, green, and pink. You'll find these earth stars especially effective in small dish gardens and in bottle gardens.

The billbergias, epiphytic bromeliads with their upright rosettes of rather narrow leaves, are old favorites with indoor gardeners. One of these, *Billbergia nutans*, is called queen's tears because its small tubular flowers of red, green, and yellow produce a sort of teardrop. A more striking plant is *Billbergia windii*, with its large, cerise flower leaf behind a drooping flower head.

You might like to try the aechmeas, air plants that you can grow in pots. *Aechmea fasciata* is one of the favorites, with broad, silvery banded leaves and a fascinating club-shaped flower that starts pink and gradually changes to blue as it ages. The flower goes on for months. The rosette may reach from 18 to 24 inches across. Don't forget to keep its vase filled with water.

A bit more dramatic is *Vriesea splendens*. In general shape it's much the same as the aechmeas. It's the leaves that are different—green with dark bands. Out of the center grows a narrow bright red spike—which gives it its other name, flaming sword—from which little yellow flowers peer out. A really handsome vriesea is *V. hieroglyphica*. It has dark stippled markings, like mysterious writings on light green leaves.

A great flat wheel of a plant like the epiphytic *Neoregelia carolinae* might appeal to you, perhaps. Look for the cream and pink striped "Tricolor" form. Tiny blue flowers appear in the center, which must be filled with water although it doesn't look like a vase plant.

Nidularium innocentii is similar to the neoregelia. This one has olive green leaves, which form a nestlike rosette of bright red near the center, where white flowers form.

If space is your problem there are the guzmanias, smaller plants that send up leafy flower heads of bright orange on short stems. The pendulous Spanish moss is well known to those who live in the southern states where it can be seen sometimes growing on telephone wires. This is an epiphytic bromeliad too—*Tillandsia usneoides*. If you have a humid room you can start off one of these plants; just fix it to a piece of wood and it will grow. Keep it well misted. The same treatment applies to other tillandsias you may choose. They are all quite small but their rosettes are more distinct than Spanish moss. *Tillandsia cyanea* and *Tillandsia lindenii* are the most popular, and have a beautiful pink flower spike with bright blue flowers. Grow these two in pots in the usual way.

Above: The multicolored flowers of *Billbergia nutans* give it the name queen's tears because nectar trickles from them to form a teardrop.

Left: One of the most popular bromeliads is *Aechmea fasciata*. The rosette can reach two feet across and the flower head lasts many months.

Right: One of the smaller bromeliads is *Tillandsia cyanea*, which produces a large flat flower head from quite small rosettes.

Cacti and Succulents

We all have favorite plants; and, if we are successful with them, what better reason is there for specializing. Cacti—and the succulents that resemble them—seem to come out high on the specializing list. It's also a fact that you don't often find someone with a very mixed collection of plants who includes any cacti among them. You either love cacti, it seems, or you hate them. If you love them, you can't have enough of them.

As it happens there are literally thousands of cacti and succulents to choose from, so there should be enough to satisfy even the most avid collector. With such a bewildering choice, then, let's take a broad look at some of the kinds you can expect to meet, their needs, and some of the pitfalls.

But before you even start your collection perhaps we should ask the questions "What exactly is a cactus, and what are succulents?" Most cacti have no leaves, or, where they do, they are very small and of no importance. One striking characteristic of cacti is the fact that they nearly all have spines, or bristles, which can be colored and arranged in patterns. Sometimes they have a matting of fine hairs, often in a form that looks like felt or wool. They are mainly round or cylindrical plants, although there are other shapes, too, such as the flat pads of prickly pears.

Above left: Small cacti are particularly attractive when grouped together, especially when in flower.
Above: Smooth-leaved succulents, mainly echeverias, transform a shallow bowl into a miniature garden.

Unlike cacti, other succulents do not belong to a single family, but all are plants that have developed fleshy, water-retaining leaves or stems and can live through periods of hot, dry weather without any additional moisture. They don't usually have spines. Some form rosettes; some grow upright like cacti and have no leaves; others have fleshy leaves of various shapes on erect or trailing stems. They come in all sorts of colors, too: browns and blue-greens for instance, and quite a few are "woolly." It's not being too unkind to say they all look a bit bizarre. Some, though, are startlingly attractive—and, as they say, beauty is in the eye of the beholder!

You should find cacti and succulents quite easy to look after in your home. Their most important need is bright sunlight, and plenty of it. Put them on any sunny windowsill, or table or shelf as near the window as you can get it; and turn the pots around regularly so that the plants get sun on every part. They also like to be kept warm and dry so dispense with the pebble trays and the mist-sprayer; unlike most leafy house plants, they love a dry atmosphere—the drier the better. This doesn't mean that you can forget to water them. They do need water, although they're able to survive with very little. Do give them plenty to drink in summer when they're growing, however. The best time to water is either early morning or late afternoon. In fact, before or after the sun gets really hot. A word of warning here: take care that no water is left on the plants: the drops can act like magnifying glasses so even quite weak sunshine can scorch the plants and leave ugly marks. Water only when the soil begins to dry out: check how far the pot has dried out by scraping away a little of the topsoil and feeling underneath. Often, you'll find that the soil is damp an inch or so below the surface. If you have to probe deeper, then it's time to water.

Never let succulents remain in wet soil. They hate this and become limp and look really sick. After all, nature has adapted them to store moisture for survival in very dry desert conditions—they won't be able to cope with your generosity.

In winter keep cacti and succulents very dry, watering only enough to stop the soil drying out entirely. If ever you're in doubt about watering succulents, don't! It's also important to remember that succulents are tender, so don't leave them where they may get damaged by frost—they probably won't recover.

Most of the cacti and other succulents suitable for your home are easy to grow. Unfortunately, most of them have difficult-looking scientific names. Many have popular names, too, and as they're usually very descriptive, we'll give them as well. Some-

Right: Yellow-flowered *Rebutia kesselringiana* with red peanut cactus, *Chamaecereus sylvestrii.*

Below: Most mammillarias make neat round plants that flower young, like *Mammillaria zeilmanniana.*

Right: Few prickly pears bloom readily in pots, but *Opuntia compressa* is an exception. It should be grown in a reasonably large pot.

Above: The jade tree, *Crassula portulacea*, makes a large bush covered, in time, with white flowers.
Left: Echeverias such as *Echeveria glauca* are very easy to grow and produce many offsets around the stem, which will root if taken off and repotted.

times, though, two or more quite different plants have the same popular name. It's safer, then, to order by their scientific name if you're to be sure of getting what you want.

Some cacti produce lovely, impressive flowers quite readily. For big, shiny blooms with many petals and stamens ask your nurseryman to show you the rebutias, lobivias, parodias, and the peanut cactus, *Chamaecereus sylvestrii*. If you want something especially interesting try the globular cacti, which include the mammillarias with such descriptive names as powder puff and old lady cactus. Among tall upright ones are various cereus, such as the night-flowering Peruvian torch (*Cereus peruvianus*). The young ones are fine as indoor plants but they eventually become tree-sized if you keep them long enough. The notocacti—with names like scarlet ball, silver ball, Indian head, and Paraguay ball—produce large flowers that, alas, last for only a day. The spineless, silvery astrophytums have four or five chunky segments that suggest their popular names like bishop's cap, sea urchin, star cactus, and goat-horn cactus. Woolly-haired ones include the old man cactus, *Cephalocereus senilis*—you'll have to give this one a shampoo if it gets grubby! A popular cactus, that sometimes has a rabbit silhouette, is bunny ears, *Opuntia microdasys*, one of the prickly pears. Don't stroke it because the

Above: "Living stones" such as *Lithops olivacea* are extraordinary succulents needing a good deal of care, very sandy soil, and limited watering.
Below: *Kalanchoe pumila* is one of a large group of easy succulents that flower freely.

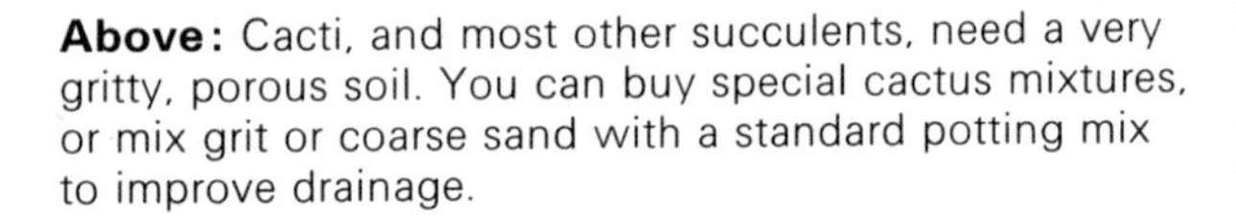

Above: Cacti, and most other succulents, need a very gritty, porous soil. You can buy special cactus mixtures, or mix grit or coarse sand with a standard potting mix to improve drainage.

Above right: When repotting choose a clay pot only a little larger than the old one, and cover the drain hole with pot shards.

Right: Avoid the sharp spines by folding a piece of newspaper into a narrow band around the plant.

"ears" are packed with tiny prickles.

If the prickly types aren't your thing you can still have all the variety, oddity, and color found in cacti by choosing succulents. Among those to look for are the echeverias. They are rosette plants, mostly blue-green and sometimes furry, which often produce lovely waxy bell-shaped flowers. Other attractive rosette plants are the aloes, such as the partridge-breast aloe *Aloe variegata*, with stiff leaves of mottled green and pinkish-orange flowers. A definitely spiky rosette is formed by the tiger's jaws (*Faucaria tigrina*). Its thick, triangular leaves have toothlike spines along the edges. It also has pretty yellow flowers. Look, too, for the spreading, pendulous kinds of crassula, with fleshy leaves threaded like beads on their thin stems. Other kinds, such as *Crassula argentea*, make neat tree-shaped plants with glossy leaves. Striking carmine flowers are carried by *C. falcata*, which has curiously shaped flattish leaves pressed against the stem.

The small, starlike flowers of many of the sedums are just one of the attractions of this big group, which has kinds that range from tiny trailing plants to shrublike upright ones. Their fleshy leaves vary in shape and color, some with long, rounded, or flattened leaves, some in glossy reds and browns. For an attractive basket plant try the donkey tail, *Sedum morganianum*. It has yellow-green close-packed leaves on long trailing stems. Place a pot of it on a stand, or hang one on a wall for the best effect.

Baby plants complete with roots appear on the leafy edges of the maternity plant, *Kalanchoe* (or *Bryophyllum*) *daigremontianum*. Clusters of orange, red, yellow, and salmon blossoms make kalanchoes very popular con-

Left: After removing the cactus from its original pot with the aid of the paper, transfer it into the new pot, in which some soil mix has been placed.

Below left: Fill with soil and press down very firmly around the cactus with a suitable tool.

Below: A layer of grit or stone chippings on top of the soil not only looks attractive but also helps to avoid rotting because the grit forms a dry "collar" around the base of the plant.

tributors to dish gardens. Among the most unusual of all the succulents are the knobbly "pebble plants" (*Lithops*). These curious little plants never fail to interest their growers, and are always a great attraction to friends. Although difficult to grow they are worth a try—give them maximum sun.

Bright green leaves among long spines and handsome, long-lasting orange-red flowers have made the crown of thorns (*Euphorbia splendens*, sometimes called *E. milii* or *E. bojeri*) the most popular of the large family of succulent spurges (euphorbia).

At some time your cacti and succulents will need repotting. Remembering how we repotted ordinary house plants, you may ask, "Just how am I supposed to hold a cactus when it's covered with spines?" Well, the solution to that is quite simple. Either wear thick gloves or use a piece of folded newspaper. Use the newspaper to encircle the base of the plant. You can have a firm hold on the plant without getting scratched.

All cacti and succulents need to be planted in very porous soil. You can easily adapt ordinary potting soil by adding one part grit or coarse sand to every four parts of potting soil. Alternatively, you could buy this already made up. Peat-based potting mixes are not really suitable for succulents. If you want to make your own, use seven parts loam, three parts peat, four parts coarse sand, or grit.

Repot your succulents by following the same tapping-out routine you used for ordinary house plants, holding cacti in gloved hands or newspaper. Pick away some of the old soil from the roots. Check all over for rot and pests—discolored stems, deformed new growth and swellings on roots. If you see any of these danger signs look for the remedy under "There's Bound to Be Trouble" (pages 130–133) later in the book. Lastly, remove any dead roots. When selecting a new pot make sure that it's only slightly larger than the old with a little extra space to spare for the roots. Try to use clay pots if you're in any doubt about watering. They're porous enough to get rid of excess water if you should be overgenerous with the watering pot occasionally.

So, if your new pot is a clay one, cover the drainage hole with pot shards first, and then put in a layer of stone chippings. If it's a plastic pot, or some other material, go straight ahead with the chippings. Put an inch or so of soil into the bottom, hold the plant in the center of the pot and gradually trickle fresh soil in and around the plant's roots, firming it down occasionally with a stick. The soil should be firm but not rammed in, and should be about half an inch below the rim of the pot. Cover the roots to the same level as before. Finally, sprinkle a layer of grit on the top of the soil, which not only looks nice but stops the top getting too compressed and hard.

One of the joys of your succulent collection is that you can easily increase your favorites. The best time to begin is during the warm months when the new growth begins to appear. Always use a sharp knife or razor blade to make cuts and then leave the cutting in a warm dry place for at least two or three days until a sort of new skin, or callus, forms over the cut surface. When the cutting has callused place it into its rooting pot; just a light push will do. Prop it up with small sticks if it won't stand up.

There are various ways you can start off your new plants, depending on the kind of succulent you want to propagate from. You can make quite large new plants by taking cuttings of branches from the branch-type cacti. Those with youngsters (offsets) at the base are simple to propagate. Just separate them from the parent plant and pot into sandy soil. Cut off the pads of prickly pear and root them when they've callused. If the cacti is one of the long cylindrical ones, cut it into horizontal sections and, after drying, insert in sandy soil but keeping the pieces the same way up as they were when growing.

Right: The varied shapes of succulents are best appreciated when they are grouped into containers. Here, in a container without drainage holes, smallish plants in their pots have been placed in gritty soil on a thick bed of pot shards.

Below: The echeverias readily produce delightful little vase-shaped flowers. A clustering plant in an attractive container forms a lovely desktop decoration with the little figure.

To increase stem-forming succulents, cut off a section of the stem with some of its leaves; rosette plants with very short stems need cutting just below the rosette. Short rosette plants produce lots of offsets that you can detach. Many succulents, such as crassulas and sedums, can be grown from single leaves.

The best material for rooting is a mixture of coarse sand and peat in equal parts. Keep this moist but not soggy.

Once the cutting has roots of reasonable size you must move it into a pot of the soil

mixture we described because there is no food in peat, sand, or vermiculite.

You'll find that once you've started your collection of succulents, you'll want to go on adding and adding. But as they really need windowsills, you'll soon find you have long rows of pots everywhere. If it appeals to you, one way out of this dilemma is to build two or three shelves across suitable sunny windows—glass shelves work particularly well.

If you're in any way artistic then you'll probably get a lot of satisfaction arranging your plants in groups. All the varied shapes and colors of succulents—even of cacti alone—make it very easy to compose attractive associations. Why not try landscape gardening in miniature? There are many small succulents that can form the vegetation in, say, Japanese-style miniature gardens. You can even add tiny pagodas and bridges.

Grouping your plants means putting them together in a suitable container. Those sold for dish gardening are ideal—you should be able to get square or oblong ones three or four inches deep. But these are not to everyone's taste. In any case, they have drainage holes, which means putting them on a plate or drip tray to prevent moisture oozing out and spoiling your furniture.

Don't be afraid of using glazed bowls, dishes, or any deeper containers you may have. The important thing to remember

Above: The orchid cacti or epiphyllums produce huge, sumptuous flowers. The silky blooms, with large numbers of petals and stamens, spring from long leaflike stems.

is that the soil must be well-drained.

If your container doesn't have a drainage hole then put a thick layer of pot shards and gravel at the bottom so that surplus water can be kept well away from the soil and the plant roots—and always water with care.

When you choose the plants for your dish try to put together only those that have similar needs. You're heading for trouble if you put one plant that doesn't need much water with others that need considerably more—you'll probably end up by spoiling all of them!

Start your display collection by putting a thick layer of special gritty succulent soil mix on top of the layer of pot shards and gravel. Ease the plants one by one from their old pots and plant them carefully but firmly in the soil. Remember to space them out fairly well to allow for some growth. You can then camouflage the soil with grit, attractive stones, or shells.

Alternatively, you could fill the dish with clean sand and bury the plants in it in their original little pots so that the top of the soil is just covered. This stops the roots of the plants getting entangled, which can lead to trouble when eventually you have to separate them—for sooner or later the plants will get crowded.

Be particularly careful when watering any succulent arrangement in a dish with no water outlet because any surplus water is likely to kill the plant roots and cause rotting. Every now and then tip the bowl carefully to drain the excess water. Even so, you'll be surprised how much water will be used up in summer, whereas in winter, the plants survive on very little moisture.

There is a group of cacti that is quite different from all the others. This group is found in humid jungles and needs very different conditions than the dry air and sunlight required by the spiny desert types.

These jungle dwellers like moist air, filtered light, and warmth, like many other house plants. At the same time they will put up with unsuitable conditions and a bit of neglect. Plants in this group have what appear to be leaves, though in fact they are really flattened stems. Their great attraction, however, is undoubtedly the beautiful flowers they produce—up to a foot across in some cases. So, if you like something exotic, these cacti are for you.

The group with the showiest flowers are the epiphyllums, or orchid cacti. In late spring the long, wavy-edged stems carry enormous blooms, with masses of shiny petals and a cluster of fine stamens, in shades of pink, mauve, cream, and white.

If you can get hold of it, a smaller relation called *Nopalxochia* is equally striking with masses of shell pink flowers, which it produces very regularly.

The Christmas cactus *(Schlumbergera*, or *Zygocactus*, *buckleyi*) has long, rather narrow cherry-red flowers. It is a pendulous plant with short, notched stem segments. The crab or Thanksgiving cactus *(Schlumbergera*, or *Zygocactus*, *truncata)* looks similar to the

Christmas cactus but produces flowers earlier. There are hybrids and varieties with white, pink and orange flowers.

There is also a smaller relation, *Rhipsalidopsis gaertneri*, sometimes called Easter cactus, which is very free-flowering with smallish, multipetaled, bright-red flowers.

You should pot these jungle cacti in a fairly rich soil, say two parts loam, one part peat and one part coarse sand, with a good sprinkling of a balanced granular fertilizer. Alternatively, they can go into one of the peat-based potting mixes, but then as soon as the buds start to form you must feed them once every three weeks with a fertilizer high in potash.

When the buds show on these plants keep the temperature around 65°F. *Don't* turn or move the plants as the buds grow, or they will fall off.

Whatever kind of jungle cactus you choose, try to follow its particular growth pattern if you want flowers regularly. With an epiphyllum, for instance, cut down watering for four to six weeks after flowering. Put it outside in summer, if possible, but out of the scorching sun. Water and mist-spray regularly. Before any danger of frost bring it indoors and keep almost dry until buds form. As soon as you see the buds forming start watering again, keeping the soil nicely moist.

Christmas cactus needs its "rest," too. From late August until buds form give just enough water to stop the leaves looking shriveled. Crab cactus should rest cool and dry until November—it can flower for Thanksgiving and sometimes goes by the name of Thanksgiving cactus. Easter cactus needs less of a distinct rest. In each case a cool place is best during the rest period.

You can propagate all these jungle cacti by taking off a bit of stem, say three or four segments, or "leaves." Give the stem three days to dry the cut, then push the bottom segment part-way into moist peat. With orchid cacti a single long segment is enough; it should have the lower quarter cut off, and the cut allowed to dry.

This is, of course, only a brief glance into the world of cacti and succulents but we hope it will encourage you to try your hand at growing these unusual and rewarding plants.

Above: The crab cactus *Schlumbergera truncata* and the similar Christmas cactus usually have red flowers, but look for other shades.
Left: Tongue-twisting *Rhipsalidopsis gaertneri* produces a profusion of blooms around Easter.

Ferns for Shady Corners

Most of the house plants you are likely to buy will at some time produce flowers. They may be insignificant ones in some cases, but at least the plants are capable of blooming. Ferns, on the other hand, don't flower. (As it happens, in the evolutionary time scale ferns developed long before flowering plants.) However, what they lack in blossom is more than made up for by their grace and beauty.

There are lots of handsome ferns to choose from and it's very tempting to collect as many as you can possibly fit into your home. One of their most useful qualities is their versatility. They can give just that feeling of coolness and tranquillity you may want to create in a certain spot. They can also give a touch of movie-star glamour and luxury—try surrounding your bathtub with them. You'll feel as though you're bathing in a pool in some faraway jungle.

You'll find the easiest ferns to keep are those with hard, leathery leaves, such as the holly fern, *Cyrtomium falcatum*. Its dark green leaves resemble holly but without the prickles, and are so shiny they look as if they'd just been polished. This fern will put up with drafty corridors and the darkest corners of a room. It will also stand low winter temperatures. The charming, neat roundleaf or button fern, *Pellaea rotundifolia*, with round dark green leaves, is also fairly tough, and is attractive in bottle gardens.

A really good general-purpose fern is the attractive Boston fern, *Nephrolepis exaltata*. It has long, wide, rich green feathery fronds, very graceful and slightly arching, and is available in many varieties.

Almost equally easy are the *Pteris* ferns. There are lots of different kinds—such as brake, ribbon, table, and Victoria ferns—that will grow very well indoors. All have attractive strap-shaped leaves, plain green or with white or silver variegation and often cut or crested at the tips. The best known is the ribbon fern, *Pteris cretica*.

The maidenhair ferns, or adiantums, are practically everyone's favorites. Their delicate, fan-shaped leaflets make up fronds that quiver gently in the slightest breath of air. Unfortunately, they're temperamental in ordinary home conditions, and wither at the merest hint of dry air or draft. If you seem to have found the perfect place for them then don't move them—you're in luck. An easy one is *Adiantum cuneatum*.

Something of a curiosity are the davallias, such as *D. bullata*, *D. fijiensis* and *D. trichomanoides*. They have creeping overground stems, or rhizomes, covered with what looks like brown fur, giving them the names rabbit's-foot or squirrel's-foot ferns. Their stems will eventually spread over the edge of the pot and creep down it, which makes them effective hanging-basket or pedestal plants. The davallias have the normal, feathery dark green fronds. Another fern with stems resembling animals' feet is the hare's-foot fern, *Polypodium aureum*, which has handsome bluish fronds cut into a few wide segments.

Asplenium bulbiferum, mother fern or mother spleenwort, has the typical graceful ferny look. You'll be fascinated by the masses of young plants it produces along its fronds. When they're large enough to grasp easily, carefully pull the youngsters off and press them into small pots to make new plants. The related *A. nidus*, or bird's nest fern, is

Above: The mixed ferns seen here are growing in a Wardian case—a Victorian version of the terrariums described later. Such cases are now very rare: this one was saved from a junkyard by the authors. It makes a perfect fernery.

quite different. It has bright green uncut fronds radiating from a central point. The fronds can be anything from six inches to three feet long. Try to find the forms with black midribs, because they will stand the lowest temperature. Sensitive to hot dry air, they're best kept on humidity trays.

Another distinctive fern is one of the so-called "hard" ferns, *Blechnum gibbum*. It forms a graceful rosette of broad, equally divided, leathery fronds. As it matures it forms a thick stump like a tree trunk.

The most extraordinary of all the ferns is one that looks just like a set of green antlers, *Platycerium bifurcatum*, the staghorn fern. This is an epiphyte and the large rounded fronds at its base clasp the tree branches on which it lives. From these fronds sprout the "antlers," some as long as two feet.

If you'd like to try one of these unusual ferns they're best grown wired to a piece of cork bark with plenty of sphagnum moss behind the round fronds. You can grow them equally well in a clay pot. Just see that the round fronds curl around the rim yet still leave space to get at the soil for watering.

Ferns, like all other plants, need some light in order to grow, but as woods and

Above: The Boston fern, *Nephrolepis exaltata*, with its long, rich green fronds, is both very graceful and easy to grow, putting up with all kinds of treatment. Here it is at home in an unusual holder: the weighing pan of an antique scales.

Below: One of the neatest ferns is *Pellaea rotundifolia*, which gets its name of roundleaf or button fern for obvious reasons. It is excellent in bottle gardens and good in most indoor conditions, though it won't stand full sun.

rocky clefts are their natural habitats, they can flourish in fairly dim corners. What they don't need is bright or strong light, least of all sunlight, so keep them well away from sunny windowsills. Although many ferns will live quite happily in a cool spot, there are many others that can be placed almost anywhere in your apartment or house, and in almost any temperature. Don't leave them in a hot dry atmosphere, though. They hate it. In winter keep your ferns cool, between 50° and 65°F.

Ferns thrive when they are kept moist. This always carries a danger of overwatering, so be careful. They must never be allowed to stand in water nor, on the other hand, to dry out completely; either will do enormous damage. Water quite freely during the growing season, when you can also give them liquid fertilizer every two months from May to September. The best way to give your plants the humidity they love is to stand the pots on pebbles in trays of water, or sink them in dishes of moist peat and mist them daily with tepid water. Dry air will quickly wither the ends of the fronds.

When repotting is necessary, follow the same rules as for ordinary house plants: place your hand across the top of the pot, plant stem between your fingers, turn the pot upside-down and knock the pot rim on a ledge until it slides off the root ball. Be extra careful how you handle the root ball as ferns are particularly sensitive to root damage. As the fine, dense roots dislike being pot-bound, try to make it a rule to repot your ferns every year. A good potting mixture can be made from equal parts of peat, fine leaf mold, and loamy soil, but a standard peat-based one will do just as well. Never repot into pots more than half an inch bigger than the root ball because too much extra soil may go "sour."

The best way to increase your favorite ferns is by division. Division is a matter of pulling the root ball apart as gently as you can. If it won't divide, use a sharp knife.

Incidentally, ferns reproduce from spores, which are produced in tiny sacs that look

like brown spots on the underside of the leaf fronds. Don't be misled by these into thinking your ferns have some disease!

Maybe you've got a well-lighted window box that would be improved by some fern and you aren't sure how the traditional filtered-light-loving ferns would react? Then try some of the so-called "ferns" that aren't really ferns at all but, unexpectedly, members of the lily family. The most widely known of these is the asparagus fern, *Asparagus plumosus*, a very lacy-looking, feathery-leaved plant with long wiry arching stems. *A. sprengeri*, or emerald feather, has a much looser make-up and small narrow leaves; it is basically a climber but you'll find it will sprawl happily out of a hanging basket to great effect. If you want something neater then try *A. meyersii*, plume or foxtail asparagus, which has erect stems up to 12 inches long with hundreds of narrow leaves.

Do remember that these plants are not ferns, so they'll need well-lit conditions and rather less humidity.

Above: *Pteris cretica*, one member of the big pteris family, variously called brake, ribbon, table or Victoria ferns.
Below: A young specimen of the extraordinary staghorn fern, *Platycerium bifurcatum*.

Below: The asparagus fern, *Asparagus plumosus*, gets its name from its feathery leaves on long trailing stems; but it is not really a fern at all—it belongs to the lily family. It should be given stronger light and drier conditions than true ferns.

Exotics Made Easy

How many times, as you walk around a nursery or florist shop, do you find yourself drawn toward the unusual, and often enchanting, exotic plants? Although they are really greenhouse inhabitants that demand a constantly moist atmosphere and a narrow range of temperatures, you can probably grow them in your home if you're prepared to take a little trouble.

One of the main requirements of exotic plants is that they must have a layer of constantly moist air around them. The best way to provide this humidity is to stand their pots on pebbles in fairly deep trays filled with water to just below the pot bottoms—and mist frequently. Apart from these general instructions each species and variety has its own rather special needs, so we'll deal one by one with some of the more tempting of these.

Among the exotics, caladiums are the only ones that don't flower, but the magnificence of their foliage more than makes up for their lack of flowers. The large, roughly heart-shaped leaves in incredible colors are very striking. Some varieties are white with green veins, others add various tones of red and pink to green and white, and some look as though they're made of red-hot metal. But the leaves are paper-thin and wither easily in dry air. Caladiums are tuberous, and like all plants with underground storage organs they have a period of rest followed by a period of active growth. When the caladium leaves start to die down, reduce the water supply and, when they're dead, keep the pots quite dry, but warm. In February, empty out the pot, pick out the tubers from the soil and repot them, knobbly side up, in very peaty compost. Then start watering again and keep them warm. By March the tubers should sprout once more.

Hanging baskets of tubular, two-lipped flowers in either fiery or dull reds, orange, or in combinations with splashes of yellow are—probably—the tropical American goldfish plants, columneas. Sprouting from long hanging stems with neat paired leaves they look nothing like the African violets they're related to. Pot them in packaged African violet soil mix and place them in areas that receive bright but filtered light, never strong sunlight. Don't put them anywhere where the temperature goes below 58°F. Use tepid water for watering but don't spray the rather hairy foliage.

Even more startling are the flowers of a related plant sometimes called basket vine, or lipstick vine, aeschynanthus. The clusters of trumpet flowers at the ends of the stems emerge from their calyxes like colored lipsticks. The glossy, dark-green leaves can be sprayed, but lipstick vines are rather temperamental: too much light will turn leaves pale, and they must have warmth and humidity.

The exquisite gardenia bush usually requires greenhouse culture where it can be given the steady temperatures and the humidity it needs. Indoors, it is easy enough to keep the bush growing, but difficult to ensure that it flowers. The best place for home culture is a sun room or screened

Right: The lovely Madagascar jasmine, or stephanotis, has waxy leaves and wonderfully fragrant flowers. Here it is growing on a wire hoop, a good way to keep a fairly strong climber under control.

Above: Cascading columneas look like chains of fire. The trailing stems can reach several feet, so they are best grown in hanging baskets.
Left: Some of the most dazzling leaf colors of all come from caladiums. They're paper-thin, however, and difficult to grow in a dry atmosphere.

veranda. Generally, though, keep it a cool 60°–65°F all winter, with the roots preferably just a little warmer. Keep it that way until the buds are fat, then, around March as flowers open, give it lots of water and frequent mist-spraying. While flowering, it likes plenty of light, but not direct sun, and fresh air with temperatures as near to a steady 65°F as possible. Like most of the "special" plants, the gardenia should be watered with completely lime-free water—distilled water or rainwater—and any food must also be lime-free; for preference use an acid-based plant food.

If you need some fresh ideas for winter flowering displays try the pentas, which have rounded heads of four-petaled long-tubed flowers in pink, red, or white—and bloom from September through January. Incidentally, the Egyptian star-cluster, *Pentas lanceolata*, has been known to bloom all year. Pentas will stand a winter minimum of 57°F, which makes them useful for cool rooms. Rest them with rather less watering after they have flowered.

A wall makes a good support for growing a stephanotis—a fairly strong climber which you must often have admired in your florist shop. It is sometimes called Madagascar jasmine (*Stephanotis floribunda*). This really lovely plant, with dark green waxy leaves, will reward your care and attention with clusters of star-shaped fragrant white flowers from May through August. Even if you haven't a vacant wall, you can train the plant over a strong arch or wire frame. It's one of those plants that drops its blooms or even its glossy leaves if it's moved while in bud or flower. Apart from that, three things are likely to harm it—varying temperature (keep it around 65°–70°F), drafts, and underwatering (it can be *overwatered*, too). Mist-spray often with tepid water in the growing season, and keep an eye open for mealy bugs and scale insects, which find this very handsome plant much to their

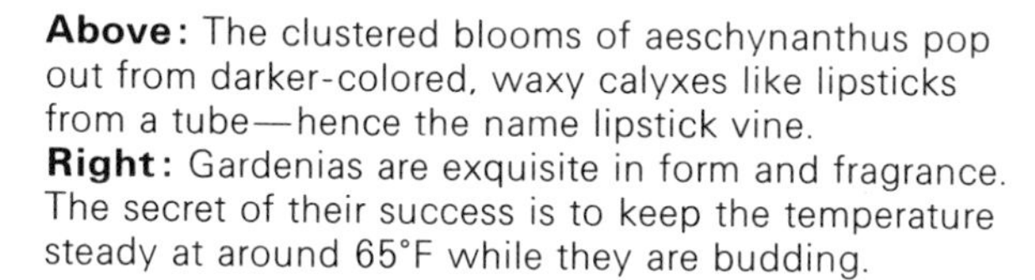

Above: The clustered blooms of aeschynanthus pop out from darker-colored, waxy calyxes like lipsticks from a tube—hence the name lipstick vine.
Right: Gardenias are exquisite in form and fragrance. The secret of their success is to keep the temperature steady at around 65°F while they are budding.

taste. (Turn to pages 130–3 for treatment of these pests.) Keep at around 55°F in winter.

Bird-of-paradise flower is the common name of strelitzia, and it well deserves it. In California and the southern states this plant will grow outside, so it is obviously fairly tough, and can survive a winter minimum of 50°F, though it's safer to keep it in temperatures a bit higher. Strelitzia's leaves are like those of a miniature banana palm, and in summer fascinating blooms of orange and violet rise from a stiff horizontal "beak"—making it look like a bird's crest. Give it good light and regular mist-spraying and it should be happy; it will appreciate generous helpings of normal house plant fertilizer in summer.

Surely the most sumptuous exotic you can possibly have in your home is an orchid. To have one flowering in your living room, say, is almost guaranteed to earn wonder and praise even from your most blasé friends.

Above: One of the most spectacular plants possible to grow indoors is the bird-of-paradise flower, *Strelitzia reginae*. It's not difficult to grow and will stand quite low winter temperatures. When not in flower the bold leaves are striking.

Left: The phalaenopsis are called moth orchids because their flat flowers look just like insects. They are among the easier orchids to grow in fairly low temperatures, and bloom for a long time.

Right: There are many kinds of odontoglossum, which vary considerably in temperature and watering requirements, so make sure you know the needs of any plant you buy.

Below left: The most common cymbidium is a tall, bulky plant, but there are now miniature varieties that grow only 15–18 inches tall.
Below: Best of the many kinds of slipper orchid for room cultivation is *Paphiopedilum insigne*, which flowers in mid-winter.

The truth is, they're not all that difficult to grow—in fact, they're tough customers if you observe their particular needs.

The most important of the orchid's needs is plenty of light: at least 10 hours a day during the growing period (most "rest" for part of the year). They are plants for windows, then: bay windows are excellent because light gets in from the sides as well as the front. If your window is facing south, screen the hot summer sun with a thin curtain of net, muslin, or similar material. East and southeast windows are excellent, as long as they get some sun.

Orchids need moist air: they hate the hot dry atmosphere created by radiators and the dehydration of air conditioners, so they will appreciate a humidity tray. And all except the steamy hothouse types enjoy fresh air on mild days. So choose a spot with temperatures of 68°–70°F where the air will be relatively moist, and go for orchids that will stand these temperatures. Orchid nurseries will be only too pleased to help you if you tell them what conditions you can provide.

Orchid pots should always be made of clay, and they must be extra well drained—fill them one-third full of pot shards. There are also special orchid pots with several large drainage holes. A good potting material is osmunda fiber, made from the roots of the royal fern, or portions of tree ferns. Another fast-draining mixture is chopped sphagnum moss and garden peat. Orchid specialists will provide these, and it's a safe rule to go on with the material your orchid starts in.

When orchids are growing actively you should water them freely, and give a daily misting.

Of the many kinds that you can grow in your home we have selected a few of the least temperamental, that are hardy under a fair range of temperatures. They all need a *maximum* winter temperature of 50°–55°F. The easiest to grow of those we've selected is *Coelogyne cristata*. It will give you many fragrant white blooms between January and April. Epidendrums have masses of small flowers in many colors. They should be allowed to dry out between waterings. The tiger orchid, *Odontoglossum grande*, has large, six-inch flowers in fall. Pay special attention to the instructions you receive with your particular odontoglossum, the temperature and watering needs of this group vary widely. The moth orchid, phalaenopsis, has sprays of pink or white flat flowers that look like moths' wings. They are easy plants if you give them medium light, and a temperature around 60°F. Finally, you'll like the slipper orchids or paphiopedilums: choose *Paphiopedilum insigne* and its varieties—they're very tough and flower in winter.

So, if someone gives you a gift of one of these exotic beauties, or if you succumb to their temptations in the store, you may well like to accept the challenge they offer and keep them as permanent house plants.

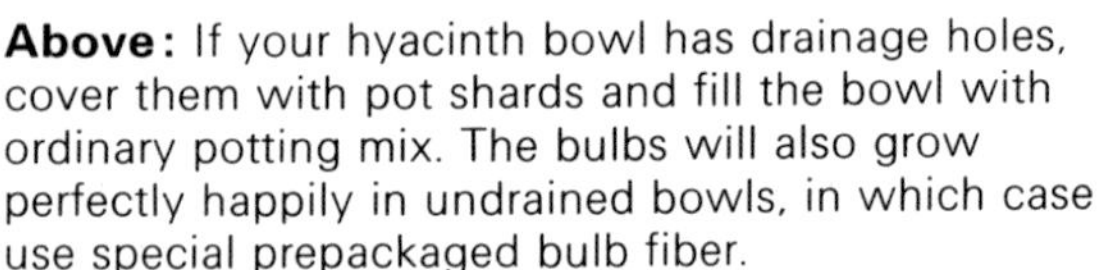

Above: If your hyacinth bowl has drainage holes, cover them with pot shards and fill the bowl with ordinary potting mix. The bulbs will also grow perfectly happily in undrained bowls, in which case use special prepackaged bulb fiber.

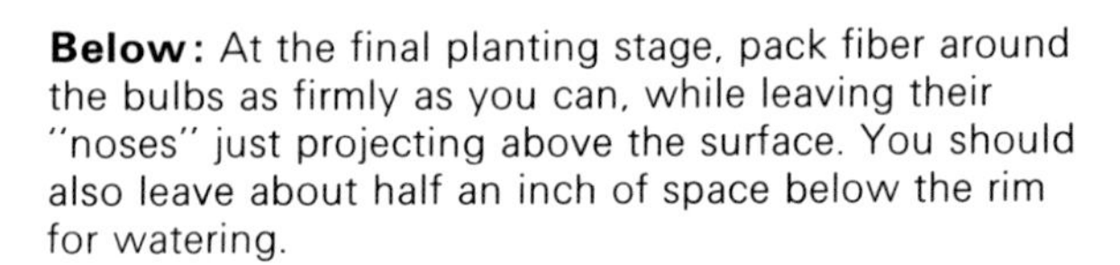

Below: At the final planting stage, pack fiber around the bulbs as firmly as you can, while leaving their "noses" just projecting above the surface. You should also leave about half an inch of space below the rim for watering.

Above: Cover the bottom of the hyacinth bowl with a thick layer of potting mix or bulb fiber—up to half the depth should be below the bulbs to allow the roots to grow. Set the bulbs upon the soil evenly spaced apart with their tops level.

Below: After setting the bulbs in their bowl they must spend eight to ten weeks in as cool a place as possible, in the dark. They should grow to at least one inch tall before being brought into a rather cool, light spot to bloom.

Beautiful Bulbs

Above: Few bulbs are more rewarding than the hyacinth. Easy to grow, in fact just about foolproof, its stocky, deliciously fragrant flowers come in a wide range of colors. As well as the standard Dutch hyacinth shown here, there are delightful miniature and multiheaded kinds.

Few things can be quite so colorful and cheering on a dull, dreary winter's day as a bowl or two full of deliciously scented, well-grown indoor bulbs. Hyacinths, daffodils, crocuses, even snowdrops and dwarf irises, can give a room a colorful, and in some cases a fragrant, accent. Easiest to grow are hyacinths, followed by daffodils and other narcissi. All you need do is follow a few simple rules and you can bring spring right into your home.

Plant your bulbs in almost any container that takes your fancy—there doesn't have to be a drainage hole in it. If the container does have a hole, put a layer of pot shards at the bottom and plant your bulbs in soil or a peat-based potting mixture. If it doesn't have a hole then use special "bulb fiber." Because the fiber mixture is very light and porous, the pot won't need a layer of shards or pebbles at the bottom. You can mix your own bulb-growing medium using six parts of peat with two parts crushed oyster shell (or other crushed shells) and one part broken charcoal (each part is measured by bulk not by weight: six handfuls of peat, two handfuls of oyster grit, one handful of charcoal). Whichever growing medium you choose, it must always be moist and cool for planting, but not wet. This may mean soaking it thoroughly, letting it drain, and then squeezing it partly dry between the hands.

Start by covering the bottom of the container with a thick layer of the bulb fiber and then sit the bulbs on it, thick end downward. At the same time try to keep all their tops level. Pack more fiber firmly around the bulbs and fill the bowl to about half an inch below the rim to allow room for watering. Leave just the tips sticking out of the fiber.

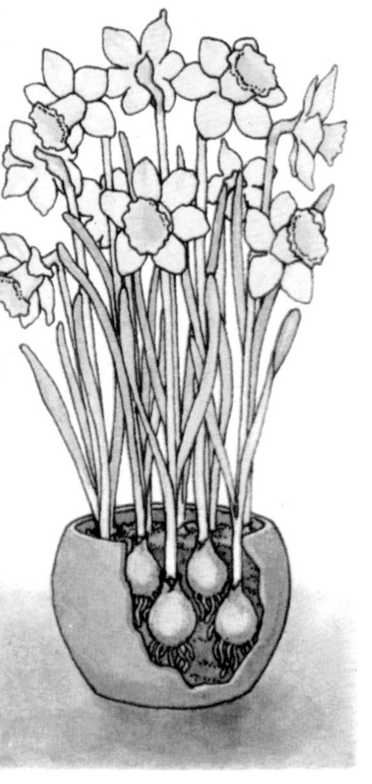

Left: For a really massed effect, grow your bulbs the multilayer way. The container must be fairly deep. Plant one layer of bulbs deep in the container and another layer above them, their bases between the tips of the first batch. Cover all with fiber and then treat in the normal way.

The next stage is important for the success of your bulbs. Always keep your bulbs *as cool as possible*—though well away from any frost—and in a dark place for at least eight weeks. A cold closet or garage would be ideal. If you live in an apartment with no really cool place available, then a balcony or window ledge outside is better than a warm spot inside.

Put the bowl of plants into a black plastic bag or cover it with lots of newspaper. Check occasionally that the fiber is still moist—if you should forget, it will quickly dry out and your bulbs won't grow.

Keep them covered until the shoots are about an inch high if they're hyacinths, about three or four inches if they're daffodils or other narcissi and tulips. When they've reached that stage uncover the bowl and bring it indoors into a cool and light place for a week or so while the flower buds push up. Keep the bulbs well watered and turn

Far left and left: Two kinds of narcissi, "Eddy Canzony" and "Gigantic Star." People often think of daffodils and narcissi as different, but the big-trumpet daffodils are just one kind of narcissus.

Below: A particularly attractive color combination in a big flat container—the dwarf tulip "Plaisir" with the brilliant blue grape hyacinth *Muscari armeniacum*. This would look best in a sun room.

the bowl occasionally so that the shoots won't lean toward the light. When the flowers begin to show move the bowl to a warmer place or wherever you want them to bloom.

If you don't like the look of brown bulb fiber, conceal it with a layer of velvety moss or sprinkle grass seed on it when the flower buds show. By the time your bulbs are in full flower they will be growing in a nice bright green carpet.

An interesting way to grow hyacinths is in a special hyacinth glass, which has a neck wide enough for the bulb to sit in. You just fill the glass with water—keep the level below the bulb, though, or the water will rot it—and add a piece or two of charcoal to keep the water "sweet." Put the hyacinth glass in a cool, though not necessarily dark, place until the roots appear and the shoot at the top has sprouted. Then bring it into the light and warmth and watch it flower.

You can buy several different varieties of hyacinths, in shades of yellow, pink, red, and blue, as well as white, all of which have a delicious fragrance. The more usual Dutch-type hyacinth has a large flower head tightly packed with blossoms. Less usual kinds include miniature hyacinths, which are small and multiflowering with graceful flower-laden spikes; and Roman hyacinths, with much more loosely set flowers that look very dainty and pretty.

For daffodils and other narcissi follow the same planting rules as you did for hyacinths. It isn't, of course, the only way to grow them. There are two interesting variations to the theme that you may like to try.

One is to grow your bulbs the "multi-layer" way. First, choose a deep container, of at least nine inches, and put in a good thick layer of potting mixture or bulb fiber. Plant a layer of bulbs and nearly cover them with fiber. Then on top of that, in between the tips of the lower layer of bulbs, put a

Above: An unusual way of growing hyacinths, especially interesting for the children, is in a hyacinth glass. Place the bulb just above water level and moisten its base to encourage the roots to start growing out into the water.

second layer of bulbs, then more fiber until you reach half an inch from the top of the container, leaving just the tips of the top layer showing. Treat the pot in the same way as your other bulbs and you should have a pot massed with beautiful blooms of varying height.

A second variation is an easy way to grow narcissi. For this you must use the "paper-white" variety, which are grown by simply pushing the bulbs into a dish of pebbles or gravel. Keep this dish partly filled with water but make sure the bulbs themselves are above it. Remove some of the pebbles now and again to check the water level—it should be close enough to the bulbs for them to absorb moisture when the roots sprout. Paperwhites don't need the usual "dark" period as other bulbs do, but they do need to

Below, left to right: Once started, hyacinth roots grow quickly and soon fill most of the glass; the leaves form a ring around the bud and finally the flower appears. Keep cool while growing.

be kept cool until the flower buds form. When the buds are ready to burst bring them into your living room to flower.

Tulips are often disappointing when raised indoors because the buds tend to shrivel, but if you like them enough to accept a challenge try those classified as early singles and early doubles. Grow them in the same way as the hyacinths but keep them in the cold for about 10 weeks. Wait until the shoots are at least four inches tall before you bring them into the light.

The most popular of the small bulbs are the crocuses, which have showy little flowers in lots of bright or subtle colors, often attractively striped. Grow them either in a pot or a shallow dish. Or, to create an especially colorful accent somewhere, grow them in a crocus jar, which is about seven inches high and has seven or eight pocket-shaped holes in its sides. You just fill the jar with damp bulb fiber and push one bulb into each pocket. Finish off by planting four or five bulbs in the open top of the jar. Keep the jar really cool and well watered until the flower buds appear. Then bring it indoors for flowering.

Several other kinds of small bulbs have extremely pretty flowers but unfortunately last only a few days when brought into a warm room. It's worth trying them, however, as they are so fresh and charming. White snowdrops, blue grape hyacinths and chionodoxas, and yellow or blue dwarf irises are just a few you could try growing. Plant them as you did the other indoor bulbs, in pots or dishes of your choice, and using potting soil or bulb fiber, but keep them cool—ideally, out of doors all the time until the flower buds are well formed. Before the buds burst, bring them into the warmth and you'll almost be able to watch them opening.

Bulbs for spring flowering in the home can be grown for only one season in a container. After that plant them out in a garden, where they will last for many years to flower beautifully each spring. For each year's indoor display you'll have to start with fresh bulbs. After having spring indoors one year, though, you'll agree it's worth the trouble it takes.

Above: Crocuses are easy to grow in pots or bowls but they must be allowed to develop buds in the cool. If possible, leave them in the garden—indoors the buds will shrivel before opening.

Below: Grape hyacinths or muscari make solid heads of tiny bell-shaped flowers, often fragrant, in blue or white; they are very easy to grow.

The idea of choosing, buying, and caring for spring bulbs only to discard them at the end of their flowering season may not appeal to you. Well, there are other bulbs you don't have to discard. These are the exotic larger bulbs which, if properly looked after, will flower regularly each year for you.

The most popular of these larger bulbs is probably the hippeastrum or amaryllis, which can have up to five enormous red, pink, white, or striped trumpet-shaped flowers at the top of a sturdy 18-inch stem, and several long straplike leaves.

Plant your amaryllis during winter (November through February). Before planting, examine the bulb's roots; if they're dry and shriveled soak the lower part of the bulb in lukewarm water for two or three days—this will help with the initial root growth. Plant it in a pot at least an inch larger in diameter than the bulb, in a prepared soil mix, or you could make a good porous soil mix of equal parts of sand, loam, and peat with an added pinch of bone meal. Pack the soil firmly around the bulb, leaving at least half the bulb above the surface.

When you've planted your amaryllis keep it warm: near a radiator or on the television cabinet is about right. Keep the soil just moist until spring, when the bud shoots up, then water more freely—it's very thirsty when in flower.

When the leaves start growing (it may be the same time as the bud, or a little later) give it plenty of light and feed it every two weeks with standard liquid fertilizer. About midsummer change to the high-potash food recommended for tomatoes. In early fall stop feeding and watering. When leaves turn yellow and dry up pull them off—it's essential for good flowers the next year. Put the bulb in its pot away in a dark closet.

From November onward watch for the first sign of green growth at the top of the bulb. When it appears, very carefully scrape away some of the old soil, and replace it with fresh rich soil. You're ready now to follow the same cycle as the year before.

Left: It's a not-quite-real experience when your amaryllis opens its enormous, satiny flowers! A good bulb should carry three or four blooms, and may sometimes produce more than one flowering stem.

Right: Nothing is easier to start off than the amaryllis (hippeastrum). Bulbs are usually sold boxed separately, and you need a flowerpot of adequate size—about six inches—and some potting mix. This bulb has just started to sprout in the box.

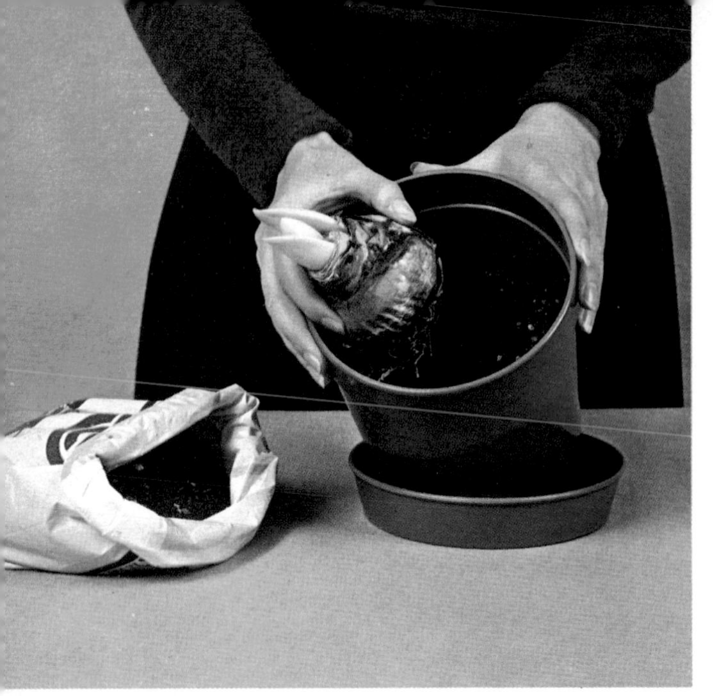

Stages in starting an amaryllis bulb.
Above left: Place the bulb on a layer of potting mix inside the pot.
Above right: Pour mix carefully around bulb.
Left: Make the mix fairly firm around the bulb, which should be left half out of the pot.
Below: Finally, water thoroughly. Then water only enough to keep pot moderately moist until bud shoots up, when more water can be given. Keep bulb warm.

Usually repotting is necessary only every two or three years because the amaryllis does best if its roots are not disturbed. Just as new growth starts is the best time to repot. Tap the bulb out of the pot and carefully wash away the soil under a gently running faucet. Repot into the new, larger pot with fresh soil to halfway up the bulb. Then plunge the whole pot into a bucket of water for about half an hour, remove, and drain off any excess water.

The Scarborough lily, or vallota, with its scarlet flowers and dark green leaves, looks like a miniature version of the amaryllis, but flowers in August and September.

Plant bulbs in June or July in prepared potting mix (choose a soil-based one if possible). Put single bulbs in pots four or five inches in diameter, or two or three bulbs in a wider pot. Leave just their necks above the soil, and water thoroughly. Then wait patiently. By August leaves and flowering stems will appear. They'll need plenty of water and sunshine and a feed of high-potash fertilizer every two weeks throughout the flowering period.

After flowering the leaves will die, so gradually reduce the amount of water you give them until about November. After that keep the soil barely moist until June or July when the whole cycle starts again. Leave vallotas in their original pots until they're truly pot-bound (which may take two or three years), then repot the same way as amaryllis bulbs.

The salmon-red flower heads of the fireball or blood lilies *Haemanthus multiflorus* and *H. katherinae* grow at the top of a long stem in the form of huge pompons made up of lots of small starry flowers with very long, yellow, pollen-tipped stamens. You plant these relatives of the amaryllis in late winter or early spring—March is a good time—in large pots of good potting soil, just deep enough to cover them. (Once potted, they won't need repotting again for several years.) Keep fairly cool and well watered and give liquid plant food once every two weeks during summer flowering. Toward the end of August gradually stop watering and let the soil dry out completely. When the leaves turn yellow and dry up, leave the bulbs to rest through the winter. When the new season's growth starts, begin watering them again, sparingly at first, and then more generously as the plants begin to grow.

The curiously attractive eucomis looks like a pineapple when it's in bloom, except that the "fruit" is a cylindrical cluster of greenish-yellow, starlike flowers topped by a rosette of small leaves. Its popular name is, in fact, pineapple flower.

To grow a pineapple flower, plant the bulb in March. Cover the bulb with moist soil in a five-inch pot. Keep moist and leave it in a cool place until it shows signs of growth. Water freely when the shoot appears and give it a liquid feed every two weeks. The flowering period is from July until September. After flowering, gradually stop watering and let the soil dry out for overwintering. The following spring scrape away some of the soil from the top of the pot and add fresh mixture. Repotting should only be done once every three to five years.

Another exotic-looking member of the lily family is veltheimia. It has glossy, crinkly-edged leaves, and between December and March produces a cluster of pale pink tubular flowers on a long freckly central stalk. Plant in September and water sparingly until the leaves begin to sprout; keep fairly cool all the time. Just enough water to dampen the soil is all the plant needs and a monthly helping of fertilizer should be ample. After flowering the leaves begin wilting, so reduce watering. By June the leaves should be dead and watering stopped. Then put the bulb away until August.

Below: Three unusual bulbs that can easily be grown in pots indoors. From left to right, the late summer Scarborough lily or vallota; summer-flowering fireball lily, *Haemanthus multiflorus*; and spring-blooming veltheimia.

Above: A single bold plant like this monstera can often be sufficient for a large room, especially if, as in this airy, well-lit setting, it is supplemented with cut flowers and dried decorations.

Left: One of the most popular of all flowering indoor plants is the patient lucy (*Impatiens*). This one makes a good contrast with the unusually shaped copper container. The combination is quite sufficient decoration for this windowsill.

Right: Almost any container that takes your fancy, whether it is a cheap plastic molding or a painted antique pot, can be made to show off a plant to advantage. Long narrow planters such as the wire-edged trough at the back are ideal for plant groups, and wooden pedestals look fine in a corner supporting a big plant in a bowl, or a climber.

Decorating with Plants

Before you buy masses of house plants take a look at how other people have integrated plants into their homes. What varieties of plants do they have, and where have they put them? What visual effect has been created in relation to room size, furnishings, and color scheme? If the plants strike the right accent and look healthy and flourishing then that's the success you should aim for.

Most plants look their best against a plain background. For a really striking effect try them against a mirror. Not only does it reflect extra light for your plants, but you get the effect of twice as many of them, for no extra cost. As a general rule, don't put distinctly marked or highly colored foliage plants against a strongly patterned wallpaper—the result will give you visual indigestion.

The decorative appearance of any house plant will be greatly improved by placing it in a handsome container.

Almost any receptacle, provided it is large enough to conceal a plain flower pot, will make a suitable decorative holder for individual potted plants. Be careful, though, for many commercially produced glazed china or clay pots will ooze moisture through onto the surface below if water is left permanently inside. You could find your table marked with a white water ring, or your carpet stained and moldy. Leaks can sometimes be prevented if you paint the inside of the pot with several coats of polyurethane. Plastic or glass containers are usually quite safe. If you should choose a wicker basket, place an old plate or saucer in the bottom to collect the drips and prevent the basket from rotting.

A number of individual plants, each in a pretty container, can be attractive either as an informal group on a tray or in a row on a windowsill—but they must match reasonably well in color. Too many separate plants, either together or scattered around a room, give a restless feeling, as well as complicating watering and other care operations.

There are plenty of containers to buy in shops but do look around the home first—your storage closet or attic may well have old china dishes and bowls, copper kitchen molds, coal scuttles—the possibilities are endless and you'll be surprised how attractive some of these objects can look filled with plants.

Arranging growing plants as a group in a planter is really very simple. First decide on size and shape and where you want to put the display, then make your choice of plants. As you choose keep in mind the plants' needs as well as growing habit. Are they sun or shade lovers? Do they need lots of water or little? Aim for variation in height as well as contrasting leaf shape, color, and texture. Remember, too, that you can use any of the flowering house plants, even temporary ones, because as soon as they're past their best you can easily remove an individual pot and replace it with something else.

If your group is going against a wall you'll need fairly tall plants at the back and lower ones nearer the front; a group for a table centerpiece will have to be fairly low growing and attractive all round.

Once you've decided on the plants you can start setting up your display group. Arrange the pots in your planter in the positions you think they look best. Leave them for a day or two to give you time to get used to it or perhaps change your mind about one or two of the plants. When you're satisfied with the grouping, remove the pots and place them on a tray in the same positions that they'll have in the planter.

Fill the bottom of the container with an inch or two of pebbles, depending on its depth. Then add about two inches of peat. Next, put the pots in position starting at the back or with the tallest plants, packing peat around the pots until they're secure and firmly embedded. When your group is complete, water the peat thoroughly. If you don't like the look of peat, you can conceal it with a layer of pebbles or neatly arranged cobblestones.

When you're watering be sure that some goes into the individual pots as well as the peat. Avoid overwatering by finger-testing each pot. If the peat becomes saturated you'll have to dismantle the display and dry it out, otherwise the whole container may smell badly after a while.

Resist the temptation to put your plants directly into a container of growing medium. You'll find that their roots will eventually grow into each other and, should you at any time want to replace one or two of the plants, it'll take far longer and be much messier than if you'd sunk your pots straight into peat.

If your container is a box choose plants of different heights and build the group into a triangular shape. For example, put taller plants on the left (or right) of the box and gradually reduce their height toward the opposite end or put a tall plant in the center and reduce the height of plants as you arrange them toward the rim. These basic triangle shapes are visually pleasing—they create a better effect than a simple straight row of plants of similar height and habit.

A window with a cheerless view can be transformed by filling the whole window area with glass shelves covered with all sorts of plants. Create your own pretty view with an indoor window box exactly the length of the sill, planted with a tall climbing plant either end, creeping up strings and with smaller plants, including trailers, toward the center.

If you have wall shelves in one of your rooms you may find they're ideal for trailing or hanging plants. Add drama at night by concealing a small light behind the plants.

You may be the lucky owner of a Victorian glazed pottery jardinière that begs to be filled with ferns or a palm. Or why not make up your own "pot-in-a-pot" stand? You'll need three large pots that fit one inside the other: fill the largest with potting soil and set trailing plants around the rim. Stand the middle-sized pot in the center, fill with soil and again set trailing plants around the rim.

Above: A very simple, functional planter has been built in near this window. The plants are growing in individual pots but have been surrounded by inert, moisture-retaining granules.

Above: An unusual living screen is created with four pots of tall-growing podocarpus, which are self-supporting. They are placed in square plastic planters which can readily be added to. The only problem with such screens in mid-room is lack of light.

Above: In the right place, a large Victorian-style multilevel plant stand displays plants perfectly and makes a marvellous conversation piece. A large plant at the top gives extra height, and some trailers blur the tray edges.

Below: A handsome Victorian pottery jardinière and stand is not only a collector's piece but a very good spot for a large arching plant like the spider plant (*Chlorophytum*) growing here.

In the center of this place the small pot, finally filling that with even more plants.

You can make your own Victorian fernery in a dull corner by arranging a group of ferns in waterproof containers on the floor around a dish of water. Alternatively, arrange them around a mirror. Conceal the edges of the mirror by putting groups of pebbles or stones among the pots themselves.

Hanging containers are always a good decorative idea for house plants. There are many kinds to choose from: those made of wire, others of plastic with built-in drip trays, or of wicker or basket with knotted string slings, or even pottery ones hanging on ropes.

You don't need many groups of plants in all shapes, sizes, and colors to create a strong visual impact. Often the most successful decor is accented by a solitary, well-chosen plant.

Some of the house plants that grow to almost tree-like proportions—rubber plants, weeping figs, African linden, and palms—can occupy an important focal position almost anywhere in your home. Your focal plant need not necessarily be a large one. The graceful aechmea—there's one called *Aechmea fasciata* with a pink flower spike and silver-dusted leaves—would catch any eye. The upright golden-edged leaves of the handsome snake plant, or sansevieria, are also very striking.

Give your room an unusual accent with a moss-filled cylinder entwined with ivies or philodendrons—it's quite easy to make and can look most attractive once the plants are established.

The best method of support for a small-leaved climbing plant such as creeping fig, *Ficus pumila*, for instance, is either a cane trellis or a wire hoop. Plants growing around a hoop can look particularly pretty. Slightly larger-leaved and more vigorous-growing plants, such as ivies, philodendrons, and scindapsus (devil's ivy), will do better growing around a moss cylinder or climbing up wires or a trellis against a wall. Ivies will grow up a wall without special support simply by using the gripping qualities of their own suckers.

To make a very effective room divider fill a floor-level planter box with philodendrons, kangaroo treebine (*Cissus antarctica*) or grape ivy (*C. rhombifolia*) and fix strings straight up to the ceiling. In almost no time at all the plants will creep upward and form a lush wall of greenery for you. Alternatively you can make a movable and slightly less tall divider by standing several pots of climbing plants in a row, each with a supporting stick.

The trailing plants (along with many of the climbing plants that can be made to trail) can also be put to very effective decorative use. For instance, if you have a shelved room divider, or a wall covered with shelves, you can instantly beautify them by placing several pots of trailing plants such as wandering jew (tradescantias and zebrinas), baby smilax and other asparagus ferns, and spider plant

Left: Unusual pottery containers hung on cords are closely grouped here, both to keep them out of the way and to form a fascinating focal point in the room. The lowest is filled with zinnias.

Below: Plants for a dining table should be low and bushy so that they do not get in the way. The flowering plant is a calceolaria.

(*Chlorophytum comosum*) at different levels to create a graceful cascade of foliage.

Trailing plants are essential in hanging baskets, of course. Groups of plants on a pedestal container look particularly good with lacy greenery trailing over the edge. In fact, any container of grouped plants will be better balanced if you drape a trailing plant over the edge at some point, visually breaking up the hard line of the container.

There are many climbing and trailing foliage plants you could use in your home. Here are a few more to add to those already mentioned: the miniature grape ivy (*Cissus striata*), purple heart (*Setcreasea purpurea*), the rosary vine or string of hearts (*Ceropegia woodii*), and of course the many forms of ivy (*Hedera helix* varieties such as "Californian," "Glacier," "Fan," and "Baltica").

To make a wire and moss "totem-pole" about three feet high you will need three or four suitable plants, approximately 3½ pounds of sphagnum moss, a piece of half-inch chicken wire measuring 11 inches by 36 inches, wire cutters, pliers, several lengths of galvanized wire, one three-inch and one eight-inch clay pot, and enough soil to fill the eight-inch pot.

Roll the length of chicken wire into a long cylinder and bind the loose rough ends of the wire together with the pliers, so that you have a continuous smooth shape. Then fill it with the moss, a little at a time, ramming it in firmly with a long stick. Fold one end of the chicken wire inward about one inch to hold the moss in place. Fold in the other end to leave just enough room to insert the three-inch pot, and push more moss around it to completely cover it. Place some pot shards in the bottom of the eight-inch pot for drainage and stand the moss-filled cylinder (with small clay pot at the top) in the center. Pour in the soil, pushing it firmly down the pot and around the cylinder, until the pot is about three-quarters full.

Next, carefully set the evenly spaced plants in the ring of soil, and then begin to wind each of them gently around and up the cylinder, securing the stems with $2\frac{1}{2}$-inch lengths of galvanized wire bent in half, as you would use a hairpin. Continue until all the plants are wound and secured around the cylinder. Gently ease out any leaves trapped under the stems. Don't worry if some of them are upside down: put the whole thing in a light place for a day or two and they will soon become oriented again. Fill the little pot, which acts

Top: Materials necessary for making a moss pole are chicken wire, sphagnum moss, potting mix—and, of course, a climbing plant.

Above: Roll the chicken wire into a cylinder and join the edges with pliers.

Left: Fill the wire cylinder with sphagnum moss, putting in a little at a time and ramming it firm with a long stick. It must be quite tightly packed.

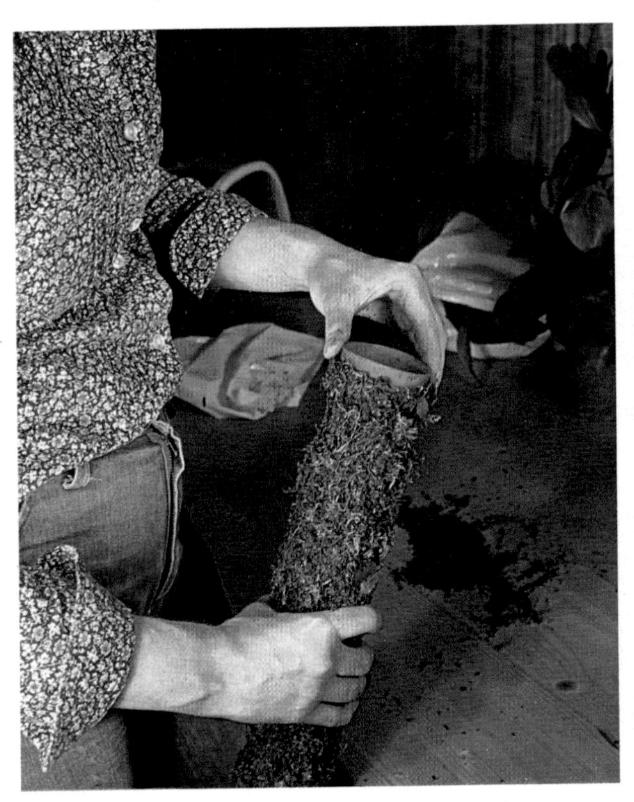

Above: Although not essential, a three-inch clay pot fitted into the top of the wire cylinder acts as a reservoir for water and helps to keep the moss damp.

as a reservoir, at the top of the cylinder with water two or three times, spray the whole column generously with water and, of course, don't forget to water the roots of the plants in the soil. Once established, fill the little pot at the top of the cylinder with water frequently, and water the large pot whenever it seems dry. The whole cylinder should be sprayed daily with water.

The cylinder may sway slightly when moved because chicken wire is flexible. If the swaying worries you, use this alternative: bind the moss thickly around a stout pole or stick using fine wire (preferably copper) and push it in the large pot full of soil. Then position your plants and train them up the moss-covered pole as you did for the cylinder. The moss pole is just as effective but may be more difficult to keep nicely moist.

Growing and caring for plants may not present too many problems for most of us. But supposing you have to go away for long periods and can't give your plants the attention they need. Or it may be that your home is too dry, or it doesn't get enough natural light, or, even, that you like a cool breezy atmosphere, which makes it too drafty for most house plants. Well, you needn't be without greenery. You can give your plants an almost perfect environment—free of drafts and with the high humidity and steady temperatures most plants love—by growing them in covered containers. These containers or "terrariums," as they're called, can be glass or plastic boxes, or glass bowls or bottles of various shapes and sizes.

This indoor-greenhouse-type gardening enables you to grow not only plants with delicate

Above: The moss pole is "planted" in the eight-inch pot and young philodendron plants are set around it. They are then twined around the pole and fixed with wire pins.

Right: The completed pole is watered by way of the small pot in the top. This reservoir will soon be partly hidden as the climbers grow up and over the top of the pole.

Left: The bottle, plants, growing materials and tools are assembled ready for planting a bottle garden. It is essential that the bottle is carefully cleaned and rinsed out first, particularly if it has ever been used to carry harmful acids.

KEY

1 10-gallon glass carboy
2 Cardboard tube to insert soil
3 Planting plan
4 Charcoal pieces
5 Pot shards
6 Soil mix
7 Wire-loop planting tool
8 Sharpened spiking tool
9 Teaspoon digging tool
10 Bobbin-stick firming tool
11 Razor-blade cutting tool
12 Sponge cleaning tool
13 Wooden lath for general use
14 *Pilea cadierei*
15 *Hedera* "Glacier"
16 *Adiantum* (maidenhair fern)
17 *Dracaena sanderiana*
18 *Euonymus japonicus*
19 *Cryptanthus bivittatus*
20 *Fittonia argyroneura* miniature form
21 *Dracaena* "Rededge"
22 *Chamaedorea elegans*

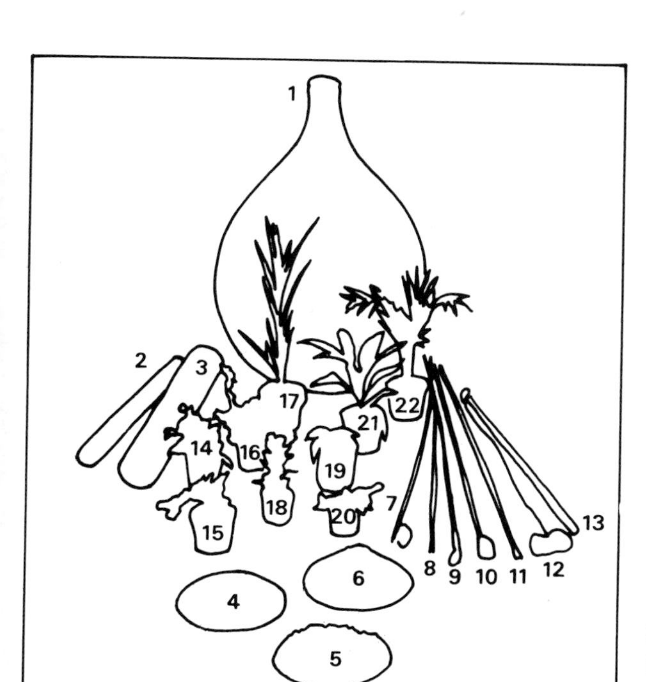

greenery and flowers, but more unusual plants such as the insect-eating sundew. You could create your own fern case using a glass or plastic aquarium with a pane of glass or acrylic for a lid. It looks particularly pretty planted with tiny ferns or other small plants. But the most elegant variation to the square terrarium is a large glass bottle—a carboy or demi-john with the basketwork removed. Whichever you use, the opening at the top should be not less than $1\frac{1}{2}$ inches in diameter.

It is quite easy to make your own bottle garden, though getting soil and plants through the top can be a little tricky. Your patience will certainly be rewarded, however, by the interest your family and friends show in the established bottle garden.

First, you need a clear glass bottle—shape and size will depend on where you want to display it—which you must clean thoroughly. Then you'll need small pieces of pot shards or gravel to make a drainage layer in the bottom of the bottle, and enough charcoal pieces to make a thin layer over the shards or gravel. Finally, you'll need soil to cover the drainage layer. The soil can be either a commercial peat-based soil mixture, or you can mix your own: one part sterilized loam, two parts fairly fine peat and one part coarse sand. Assemble your materials and fill your container. Allow a quarter of the bottle space for the soil layer. The soil layer should be made up as two-fifths drainage layer, thin layer of charcoal, then remaining three-fifths soil mixture—which should be just moist, *not* sodden.

Use a cardboard tube to pour the various materials into the bottle. The shards go in first to form the drainage layer, but to avoid them damaging the glass first pour in a little soil to break their fall. Spread each layer with a lath about an inch wide (a measuring yardstick is good for this) not forgetting the charcoal pieces between shard and soil layer. Make it firm by tamping down with a spool or bobbin fixed to the end of a long stick or bamboo cane.

The next stage is arranging the garden. Draw on a piece of paper a circle of the same diameter as the bottle at soil level. The plants you've selected can be arranged and rearranged on this until they look right—it's much better than switching them about when they're inside. If the bottle is to be viewed all around, plant the taller specimens in the center and the lower ones around them. If it will be viewed from one side only, bank up the soil a little toward the back of the bottle and put larger plants at the back and smaller ones toward the front. When you're ready to start planting begin at the outer edge of the bottle and work toward the center: in this way you'll avoid dropping soil onto any leaves.

Dig the holes deep enough to take the roots, using a teaspoon or miniature trowel fixed onto another long cane. When the hole is ready, tap the plant out of its pot and, if the roots won't go through the neck of the bottle as they are, pick away some of the soil until you can compress them into a shape that will.

Above: The first stage in planting a terrarium is to insert the various growing materials. Pour a small amount of soil into the bottle to cushion the falling pot shards; spread a layer of shards, and then one of charcoal pieces. Next pour in the remainder of the soil mix.
Below left: Using the teaspoon fixed on a cane, make a planting hole for each plant in turn.
Below center: Insert the plants with the wire loop and lower into their planting holes.
Below right: When the plant is in its hole and upright, cover the roots well and finally (bottom) make the soil quite firm around it by using the tamper.

The leaves of almost all plants should fold up enough to let you get the plant through the bottle neck.

You can buy long complicated tongs, or use wire rings fixed to a cane, to get the plants down inside the bottle. Another, simpler way, if you've got a good eye, is to tilt the bottle a little so that the plant is over the hole it's to go into—and let it drop! If it doesn't land upright ease it into the hole with the spool-cane or stick.

Be sure the roots are covered entirely and make the soil around the plant really firm by tamping it with the spool-stick. Then work in all the other plants in the same way.

When your terrarium is complete you can pour in a little water, letting it trickle down the sides of the bottle. This will also clean off any loose soil. Use very little water to start off the water cycle in your terrarium—about a cupful for a large bottle garden. The water will be used again and again as it is drawn up into the plants and transpired through the leaves. It then condenses, trickles down the sides of the bottle, and soaks back into the soil. However, keep an eye on the soil and if it looks dry pour in a cupful or two of fresh water. If you stopper the bottle you will get a lot of condensation which will obscure the plants. It's better, perhaps, to leave the bottle open and water occasionally.

From time to time a leaf will die or a flower wither, and it will have to be removed. A useful tool for cutting off dead plant material is half a safety razor blade pushed into the split end of a long cane. The blade is held firm by squeezing the ends of the cane together and binding them with tape or wire. A cane with a sharpened point is handy for spearing and lifting out plant debris.

Working with long canes in a bottle is like using long chopsticks at arm's length—a little practice and patience and you'll be surprised how maneuverable they can become.

If you're all thumbs when it comes to handling long canes, plant a terrarium in a bottle with a neck wide enough for your hand and arm to fit in, or a goldfish bowl, old candy or cracker jar—in fact almost any clear glass container will do. Large demi-john gardens make handsome lamp bases if you fix a lamp holder into a piece of cork in the neck of the bottle and fix on a large shade. Any condensation or green algal growth that forms when the bottle is corked can be wiped away with a bit of foam sponge fixed onto the end of a length of strong wire. Bend the wire into whatever shape is needed.

When you choose plants suitable for glass containers look for those that are relatively

Above: Before planting, remove soil from plant roots if they will not otherwise pass through the neck.
Right: Plants can be dropped into their holes, tilting the bottle as needed.
Far right: Two canes may be needed to get a plant exactly in place.

Left: When the bottle garden has been fully planted, any soil on the glass can be washed down by pouring a small stream of water down the side. Be careful—too much can be harmful. Use the sponge to make the soil edge neat.

Above: A delightful miniature jungle in a small plastic aquarium. The soil is camouflaged with pebbles, and a piece of glass forms the lid.

Right: Many kinds of jars, bowls, bottles, and aquariums, such as those shown here, can be used for planting. With wide-necked bottles planting is, of course, very much easier. The larger containers should be covered with a piece of glass or stiff plastic.

slow growing and then buy the smallest specimens you can. Small-leaved rex begonias look particularly pretty in a bottle and so do African violets though these are best grown in a container where you can easily take out dead blooms, which may get moldy if left. The fairly slow-growing dwarf palms are useful bottle plants, too. They give a bit of height to a group, as will a small red-brown false aralia (dizygotheca), the palmlike dracaena, and pink-edged cordyline. Small plants good as ground cover are earth stars or zebra plants (cryptanthus), mosaic or nerve plants (fittonias), and baby's tears (helxine) and the varieties of small-leaved ivies, such as "Fan," "Gold Dust," and "Maple Leaf." Other plants that grow quite happily in the enclosed atmosphere of a bottle are prayer plants (marantas)—these are ideal—the peperomias, moss ferns (selaginellas) and small maidenhair, bird's nest and pteris ferns.

One final note: don't overplant your bottle. A few well-chosen plants will look much more attractive than a bottle full of plants that look as though they're desperate for air space.

Plants from Leftovers

Left: Here is a selection from the many kinds of plants that can be grown from the seeds or roots of food plants. These were planted in February and photographed in July. At left, two peanuts, with two grapevine seedlings in front. Center front, small orange plants. Right, dates. Large leaves at back are taro yam, with sweet potato on trailing stems.

You—and your children—can have great fun growing house plants from ordinary kitchen leftovers. For instance, when you ate that orange yesterday, you threw away the seeds, remember? What a waste! You could have been one day nearer to growing your own little orange tree. Those carrot tops you chopped off and threw away—each could have produced a bright green feathery leaved plant. So ask yourself in future before you throw away any vegetable waste, "Could I grow an interesting plant from it?" Who would guess that the handsome plant growing in your kitchen was an avocado, grown from the seed, or pit, that is usually thrown away?

Every fruit you eat has seeds (unless, like the banana, they've been especially cultivated to be seedless). Sometimes they're so small you can hardly see them. Yet from these seeds you can grow some really unusual plants that cost only a little time, patience, and what you paid for the fruit or vegetable in the first place.

You can very easily grow handsome and sturdy orange, lemon, lime, grapefruit, and tangerine trees just by planting the seeds about $\frac{1}{2}$ inch deep in a small pot of damp potting soil. Then cover the top with a piece of plastic and secure with a rubber band; put the whole thing in a warm, dark spot such as a warm closet. Shoots should begin to appear in about a week or two. Do keep checking that the soil is constantly moist, otherwise the seeds will shrivel. When the shoots have formed at least two leaves, transplant your tiny fruit trees into small individual pots and keep them in a warm light place, repotting them as they grow. As they mature, your trees will produce deep green leaves and after two or three years fragrant creamy white flowers

may form, which will turn into fruits.

Give your citrus trees lots of sunshine, fresh air, and water during summer. They'll also benefit greatly from a spell outdoors at this time—provided you choose a sheltered place. In winter keep them fairly cool, away from drafts and the hot dry air that comes with central heating.

Grapes and pomegranates can also be grown from seeds following the same methods used for sprouting citrus seeds. Grape seeds produce little climbing vines with leaves and tendrils—an exact replica of the parent plant from which your original grapes were picked. Pomegranate seeds will reward you with a bushy plant of light green leaves, and in summer will put forth large, bright red flowers. Pomegranates like lots of warmth.

You can even grow a palm tree from a single date seed. Plant it about an inch deep in potting soil and keep it in a warm closet until it has germinated, just as you did with your citrus seeds—and again, keep the soil moist. After the first shoots appear—in about two months or so—put the pot in daylight. Even though it takes some years before you actually have a miniature date palm, such an unusual plant is well worth the patience.

Interesting plants can be grown from peanuts and coffee beans. Unroasted, of course. Peanuts will have to be started afresh each year, but the coffee plant is one you can keep. With its large glossy leaves and, eventually, red berries it can be a striking and tolerant room plant.

The seeds of fresh avocados, lychees, or mangoes can produce dramatically handsome plants—which seems a good excuse for eating lots of luscious fruits! Start them all off the same way, although the avocado needs a little less warmth than the other two.

Far left: A grapefruit plant about two years old and orange seedlings six months after sowing seed.
Left: Fresh peanuts sprout rapidly and make bushy plants, but these annuals last only one season.
Below: Date seeds germinate readily in moist soil in a warm place, but take a long time before they look anything like a full-grown palm tree!

Above: Avocado seeds may take some time to sprout, but will almost always grow. Once they have started, growth is rapid, and you can soon have a whole grove of the plants in various stages. Note how the roots fill the jars of water before much top growth appears.

Germinate your avocado in a small glass jar of water using three toothpicks pushed in evenly near the flat end of the seed, so that it is just below water level. Put it in a warm but shady place until the roots begin to appear; this can take up to two months, so don't lose heart. Keep the water level up so that the base of the seed is always submerged. When several roots have appeared put your avocado into potting soil leaving the pointed top quarter of an inch of the seed above the soil. You can bypass the water-and-toothpick method and start your avocado directly in a pot, pushing the seed halfway into potting mixture, which must be kept evenly damp but not sodden.

Whichever method you choose, once the first leaves have started growing, keep the plant in a warm sunny place. The way to avoid a very tall leggy plant is to pinch out the top growing point, which will encourage your avocado to bush out by forming branches. Like all your plants, you must keep it well away from drafts; also water it often and feed it occasionally during the summer.

Maybe you'd like to try your hand with lychees and mangoes. They take a bit longer to germinate, so don't lose patience. It's better to start them immediately in soil rather than to use the water method. Any large fruit seeds like these are worth a try. Some are very slow to germinate so don't throw them away until you're sure they have rotted.

You can grow many more exciting plants from your vegetable leftovers; the carrots mentioned earlier, for instance. From the

Above: Three toothpicks pushed lightly into an avocado seed support it over a jar of water (below). **Right:** Avocados can make quite big plants, but don't expect them to produce fruit indoors.

usually thrown-away tops you can grow a small plant with attractive leaves that looks like a cross between a fern and parsley. You probably remember how it's done from your kindergarten days, but in case you've forgotten: cut off the top inch or less of the carrot and stand it, cut end down, in a dish of water, adding more water when the water level goes down. You can grow leaves on beets and parsnips the same way, though of course the leaves will be different in color and shape from carrot leaves. These "plants" will usually not produce roots, but they do look pretty for several weeks, and the children love them.

Here's another simple "recipe" that will make yams or sweet potatoes quickly sprout for you. Just stand whichever of the vegetables you want to grow either in the top of a water-filled glass jar so that the base of the vegetable is under water, or plant it in a fairly big pot, covering it completely with ordinary potting mix. Give them warmth and light and don't forget to water, or nothing will happen. It is rather sad to note that in these days when almost everything is treated with some chemical or other that sweet potatoes and yams are nearly always covered with a layer of wax. If so, they won't sprout.

You'll find your sweet potatoes will grow into pretty vine-like, trailing or climbing plants with purplish flowers.

There are various kinds of yam. The irregularly oval tuber is also a climber and has attractive heart-shaped leaves. Those with cone-shaped tubers—taro or eddo—make a cluster of enormous arum lily-type leaves.

Left: This pineapple crown was carefully prepared and then placed just touching water in a jar. Roots appeared quite soon afterward. When the plant's roots reach the size shown, it is time to pot the new pineapple; otherwise the roots become too brittle for easy handling.

Below left: The rooted pineapple top has been carefully potted in a sandy soil mix. Now it will grow steadily.

Below and right: If you are lucky—and patient—the home-grown pineapple plant will eventually produce a new young pineapple in the center of its foliage.

This one must be kept very moist once it is growing.

The underground stems, or rootstocks, of ginger can also be grown into lovely plants with exotic purple and yellow flowers. Put the rootstock in a dish of water and add more as the water level goes down. When roots start to sprout, plant the rootstock in potting soil and keep it warm. Alternatively you could plant it directly into peatmoss, but you'll miss the excitement of seeing the first sprouts appear in the water. If you can buy rootstocks of turmeric—a close relative of ginger—they can be grown in the same way and are even more tropical-looking.

Perhaps you adore eating pineapples. In that case you can succumb to the temptation to gorge yourself knowing that you might be able to grow your very own fruits from the throwaway leaf stump. Slice the top off the pineapple, leaving about an inch of the fruit attached to it, then cut away the outer part, leaving the fibrous central core. Keep it in a warm and dry place to dry off completely; if you don't it may rot. When it's quite dry cut off and throw away a few of the old lower leaves and plant the crown in a damp, sandy soil mix. Keep your potted pineapple in a constantly warm—above 68°F—light place and don't overwater it (it could still rot!). If you're lucky your pineapple will take root and grow into a very handsome, if rather spiky, house plant. After a year or so your plant may produce a flower-head that will later become a fruit. Unfortunately pineapples do not produce fruits very often in ordinary house conditions.

The food we eat nowadays has so many preservatives, artificial colorings and other synthetic additives that we really do need all the natural goodness and vitamins we can get. There are, of course, lots of vitamin pills and preparations you can buy to make up any deficiency. A much more pleasant way of taking a part, at least, of your daily quota of vitamins is to grow your own from seeds. It is really quite easy and doesn't involve much

Above: The easiest method of growing vitamin-rich salad seeds is to sprout them in glass jars, rinsing them with tepid water two or three times daily.
Above right: Alfalfa, shown on the first, third and fifth days of growth.

Left: Some of the larger food roots from which attractive plants can be grown—the pink sweet potato, conical taro yam and knobbly ginger root. The resulting growth of the yam and sweet potato are among the plants shown on page 112.

work or space. Growing the vitamin-rich shoots involves creating the right conditions for seeds to germinate. This can take anything from four to seven days.

One of the easiest nutritious plants to sprout is mustard. Mustard seed takes less than a week to grow to cutting and eating stage. To grow the tiny plants simply put a sheet of blotting paper or a paper towel in a tray or plate, wet it thoroughly and then sprinkle the seed fairly generously over it. Keep it wet all the time and in a few days the sprouting seeds will be ready to eat "as is" or enjoy in a delicious crunchy salad or sandwich.

The most vitamin-rich of the sprouting seeds to grow at home is salad alfalfa, and you can germinate them either on wet paper, like mustard, or in a clear glass jar. Put the seed in a clear glass jar (four tablespoons to a 32-ounce storage jar) and cover the neck of the jar with a piece of muslin or other fine cotton cloth and fasten with a rubber band. Rinse thoroughly two or three times with tepid water—this can be done without removing the muslin cover—and keep the jar in a warm place. Rinse the seeds at least twice a day, each day, preferably morning and evening, until the shoots are ready to eat, which should be in about four days.

Chinese bean sprouts, adzuki beans, soy beans, and natural triticale (a kind of wheat) are all easy to grow either like the salad alfalfa in a glass jar or on wet blotting paper like the mustard. All the bean sprouts are ready for eating in about four or five days.

Another less usual sprouting seed for you to grow is fenugreek, which has a subtle hint of curry about it. You grow it like the others, using either the wet paper or glass jar method.

All these sprouting plants are delectable to eat raw and, of course, they're delicious cooked, too, but then they lose some of their nutritive value and their fresh, natural taste.

Increasing Your Stock

Growing indoor plants can become an absorbing hobby. You soon get to know other like-minded green-thumbers and, after admiring each other's plants, you'll naturally want to grow extra plants to exchange.

Generally the best time to begin taking cuttings, or propagating plants in other ways is spring or early summer when plant growth is at its most active.

The easiest way to propagate your plants is to divide them. Those that grow as clumps, or distinct crowns which later join together, can be cut apart. Plants that can be divided are the prayer plant or rabbit tracks (marantas) and the closely related calatheas, the cast-iron plant (aspidistra), the rushlike cyperus (keep the newer outside clumps and discard the old center clump), the Kaffir lily (clivia), African violets, and ferns. When any of these plants form a dense clump just pull it apart or, if it is very tough, use a sharp knife to split it. (The brittle African violets need care, as we described on page 63.) Kaffir lilies form groups of plants and these must be preserved, although cutting may be the only way of dealing with this lily's dense, intertwined roots. Be as careful as you can with the roots, and try to see that each of the divided pieces has a reasonable quantity of roots. Pot the divided clumps in the usual way, though with extra care where there are damaged roots. Some fine peat or a little coarse sand placed immediately around them will encourage fine roots to grow—as long as

Right: Many house plants can be increased very easily from cuttings, and soon grow into new plants for your own collection or for friends.

Left: This African violet has produced several crowns and is ready to be divided.
Above: First remove the plant from its pot.
Below: Very gently pull apart the individual crowns, taking care not to harm the roots.
Bottom: This plant produced four crowns. Now each of these is repotted and should rapidly develop into a good-sized single rosette.

you remember to keep the soil nicely moist.

Rosette-forming plants like the bromeliads reproduce themselves by growing "offsets"—young plants that sprout at ground level on the outside of the parent rosette. Other offset-forming plants are the palmlike cordylines and dracaenas, and the screw pine (pandanus). Snakeplants (sansevieria) also reproduce through offsets, although it's difficult to distinguish between a parent with offsets and a clump of plants joined at the roots. Propagation from offsets is easy. The best way is to remove the parent from its pot, scrape the soil away around the youngster, and then pull it off. Occasionally you may need to use a knife. An offset sometimes produces its own roots, so make sure you don't damage them—they give the young plant the best possible start. If an offset has not grown any roots by the time it's been separated put it into a pot containing peat, or peat and coarse sand, or vermiculite, and treat it in the same ways as the cuttings we describe later.

One important point about cuttings and plant pieces without roots: they need extra humidity to slow down the rate of water evaporation from their leaves. You can give them the extra humidity they need by placing them in a propagator or plastic bag.

There are a variety of plastic propagators you can buy, some large enough for several pots, some just a dome to fit on a single pot—or use an upturned preserve jar. A particularly cheap and easy way is to place three sticks around the edge of a pot, long enough to clear the plant pieces being rooted, put a plastic bag over them, and fasten this around the rim of the pot with a rubber band.

One of the delightful characteristics of some plants is their ability to produce miniature versions of themselves just about ready to plant. The best-known of these is probably the chlorophytum, or spider plant. Tiny rosettes of leaves sprout at intervals on the long arching stems that carry the small white flowers. In just a few weeks the rosettes will grow fat stubby roots and that is the time to make new plants from them.

Pot a rosette, still on its parent stem, into a pot of fine soil with a piece of bent wire. In a few days the roots will have grown long enough for you to separate the baby from the parent stem. If the roots are already over half an inch long, you can cut the babies from the stem and put into pots straight away. Keep them under a plastic propagator dome for a few days to speed growth.

The piggy-back plant (*Tolmiea menziesii*), has that name because new plantlets grow piggy-back fashion in the center of the older leaves. To make new plants either wait until the plantlets have produced roots, or cut off the biggest of the young plants and press them into soil in a pot, with the leaf stalk downward. Once again, rooting can be speeded up by placing the pot under a propagator.

You can root the plant known as either strawberry geranium, or strawberry begonia (*Saxifraga stolonifera*) in the same way as the spider plant. The strawberry geranium babies appear at the ends of long, fine, threadlike growths that dangle around the main plant. The little plants are not as robust as the spider plant babies so handle them carefully when trying to get them to make roots.

Baby plants appear along the older fronds of some ferns such as mother spleenwort

Above: This *Sansevieria hahni* has produced an offset from which a new plant can be grown.
Below: The offset is firmly attached to the parent rosette, and the only way of taking it off is to use a sharp knife. Cut carefully between the two plants, retaining the roots on the offset.
Bottom: Repot the offset in a small pot and it will soon grow into an attractive plant.

(*Asplenium bulbiferum*), and on a variety of the dark green leather leaf fern (*Polystichum setiferum*) called *viviparum* or *proliferum*— meaning "life-bearing" and "multiplying freely." The best way to start new plants is to pull off the larger babies and press them gently into a pot of fine, moist peat and put the pot under a propagator—or plastic bag—until the plants start forming roots.

Although succulents are very easy to root from cuttings some of them—mostly the kalanchoes or bryophyllums (botanists can't seem to agree on the naming)—make it even easier for us by producing ready-to-plant miniatures of themselves. Ask your nurseryman to show you the maternity plant (*Kalanchoe daigremontianum*), where babies form ranks along the leaf edges, and *K. tubiflorum*, where they are grouped at the ends of the cylindrical leaves. The tiny plants on *K. proliferum* are actually formed among the flowers. These kalanchoes are so profuse with infants that their pots, and any near by, usually get embarrassingly full of youngsters all begging for their own pot. You'll have no lack of something to sell or give away at your gardening club.

It's a sign of a really skillful indoor gardener when you succeed in making cuttings root—or "strike" as gardeners say. Most of the normal house plants can be increased quite easily from either stem or leaf cuttings. There are exceptions, of course, such as the thick woody-stemmed plants of the ficus family (mistletoe fig, rubber plant, weeping chinese banyan, and others), which need a great deal of heat if roots are to be produced. Many, though, root successfully from pieces pushed into a pot of suitable material—this can be a peat or prepackaged peat and sand mix. Vermiculite, and perlite too, are extremely good to root plants in. Don't forget to give them extra humidity in some way until rooting has taken place.

Let's deal with stem cuttings first. Almost any house plant with a stem can be increased from stem cuttings—usually pieces two to four

Above left: This straggly cane-stemmed, spotted-leaved *Begonia corallina* "Lucerna" has lost many leaves. Its appearance will be improved by cutting it back, which will encourage it to become more bushy. The removed stems make ideal cuttings.

Above center: Cut the begonia stems to be used as cuttings just below a "joint" or node.

Above right: Remove lower leaves, and push each cutting into a suitable rooting mix. If you use a propagator, roots will soon form.

Left: The spider plant, chlorophytum, produces ready-made young plants on the flowering stems.
Top: Peg the plantlets into small individual pots.
Above: When roots have formed and the plantlet is beginning to grow, cut off the parent stem.

inches long and taken from the ends of the stems likely to be carrying leaves. Remove all but the top four or five leaves and leave at least an inch of stem quite clear. Cut the surplus leaves off flush with the stem with a very sharp knife or a razor blade. Then push the cuttings into the rooting mixture. They can be quite close together, say five or six in a three-inch pot. Put them around the edge of the pot—it helps to keep them upright. Woody, stiff cuttings you can push into the mix without harm, but if they're soft use a pencil or piece of dowel to make a hole about one inch deep. When the cuttings are all in, press the soil around them with your fingers to make sure they are firm, and then place the pot in the propagator or plastic bag. Keep the soil fairly moist but never soggy.

It's a good sign if the propagator or bag mists up. It shows that the air is humid. Keep an eye on the cuttings, because sometimes leaves develop rot or mildew, and must be removed. Mildew and rot, both on leaves and at the base, suggest that the soil is too moist. Speed up the rooting of woody plants, such as fatshedera, by dipping the cuttings into root-forming hormone powder. It's hardly necessary to use the hormone on soft plants, such as the pileas, peperomias, stem-forming begonias, aphelandras, shrimp plant, dracaenas, or dieffenbachias. You can tell when they're rooting because the top of the stem will start to grow and new leaves may appear.

When tradescantias become leggy and lose their lower leaves, as they always do after a while, take cuttings about six inches long from the stem ends and push these into pots—they'll make new bushy growth in no time.

Many plants make roots when their stems are placed in water. It's worth trying with any plant.

A few plants are able to produce new growth from a single leaf. Among the plants that are propagated in this way are the African violet (see page 62), the related gloxinia, the peperomias and almost any succulent with leaves, such as crassulas and echeverias. To propagate these plants choose

Left: Begonias of the rex group, with thick veins on the leaf undersides, are easily propagated. **Below left:** Cut leaves into neat squares using a razor blade or scalpel, starting in the center where the veins are thickest.

Right: Lay the squares on peaty rooting soil in a seed box, taking care that they are in contact with the peat mixture. Tiny plants will soon appear on many of the squares. Alternatively, take a whole *Begonia rex* leaf, slit the veins in several places, and place on the peat. Young plants grow where the veins have been slit.

a healthy mature leaf, cut it through cleanly near the base of the stalk, and push it lightly into the same rooting mixture used for stem cuttings. Hormone powder assists rooting of leaf cuttings.

Sometimes a piece of the stem must be included with the leaf before the cutting will strike. Grape ivy (*Cissus rhombifolia*), kangaroo treebine (*C. antarctica*), cordylines, and dracaenas all strike best from leaf-and-stem cuttings. With the wax plant (hoya), look for young shoots and use just the top two leaves and a short length of stem.

In a very few cases new plants can be grown from leaf veins. *Begonia rex*, the clump-forming kind with very colorful leaves is propagated this way. Remove a leaf, turn it over and nick the thickest veins in several places with a sharp blade; then place the leaf so that the nicked veins are in contact with rooting mixture in a pot. You can weight the leaf with a small pebble to make sure it stays in place. In a few weeks little plants will appear through the leaf at each nick; the old leaf will decay and soon each new plant can be removed and potted.

Growing new snakeplants, or sansevierias, is almost absurdly simple: cut one of the long sword-shaped leaves into pieces three to four inches long and push them into rooting mixture. Quite soon they'll form roots, and, in time, new shoots will appear. One odd thing, however, is that the new plants formed from the leaf cuttings will not produce the strong yellow bands found on the edges of the kind usually sold—they're plain green. To retain the attractive yellow edge, you have to divide the sansevieria clump.

In all cases, when it's obvious the cutting has roots of its own, you can take it out of its special moist atmosphere and put it into a small pot of potting compost. It's important to do this fairly quickly because rooting substances contain little food—vermiculite none at all. If left too long in these, cuttings will get weak and may collapse.

Left: A single leaf cut from a sansevieria will provide four cuttings.
Above: Cut the leaf into pieces with a sharp knife; allow the pieces to dry out until they are calloused.

Right: Push the pieces of leaf ligntly into a suitable peaty mix, but only far enough to make them stand up.

Left: It takes time tor young sansevierias to start growing, but finally they appear from the bases of the cuttings.
Below: Turn the rooted pieces out of the pot and cut away the original old leaf pieces.
Right: Repot and water the young plants. Sansevieria cuttings cannot reproduce the original yellow leaf borders.

There's Bound to Be Trouble

Right: This imaginary plant is a guide to the possible ailments which a plant may suffer. Check the numbered symptoms with the chart on pages 132–3 and you should be able to pinpoint the trouble and take necessary action.
Above: Woolly aphis on a dizygotheca are being removed with a paint brush dipped in methylated spirit.

Just as you can't expect to get through life without an occasional cough, cold, or other mild infection (and once in a while perhaps something more serious) so your indoor plants are unlikely to go on indefinitely without health problems of one kind or another. However, apart from a few common insect pests, which you should check for as part of your regular plant-care routine, ill health in plants is seldom caused by infection. This is almost always caused by placing them in wrong locations or by faulty cultivation.

You can rarely tell at once what is wrong with a plant simply by the way it looks. If you can rule out insects, you will have to think back over the kind of treatment you're giving it and how long it's been grown that way. As with many human ailments, the symptoms almost always reflect something that has already occurred, only with plants the symptoms usually take longer to show. Those yellow leaves could be due to something that happened two or three weeks ago.

Cliché though it may be, prevention *is* much better than cure—especially with plants because few of us can spare the room to open a plant hospital. If you develop the habit of regularly inspecting your plants you'll detect symptoms of ill health at the earliest possible moment, and be able to take action before the problem has got out of hand. Similarly, if you mist-spray and wash your plants (not those with hairy leaves such as African violets or pelargoniums) fairly often, you'll find that it deters pests from making their home on the plants. Keep growing conditions right and your plants should look, and stay, healthy.

But even in the best-regulated households things do go wrong. This section is designed, then, to point out the common plant problems, the possible causes of trouble, and what you should do to put things right.

Occasionally, you may find that a plant is too sickly to restore without a long course of treatment. Have no qualms about throwing it out. The excuse for having plants in your home is that they beautify. A sickly plant that has lost its attractiveness seldom recovers, and might infect other plants.

1
2
3
4
5
6
7
8
9
10
11
12
13
14
15
16
17
18
19
20

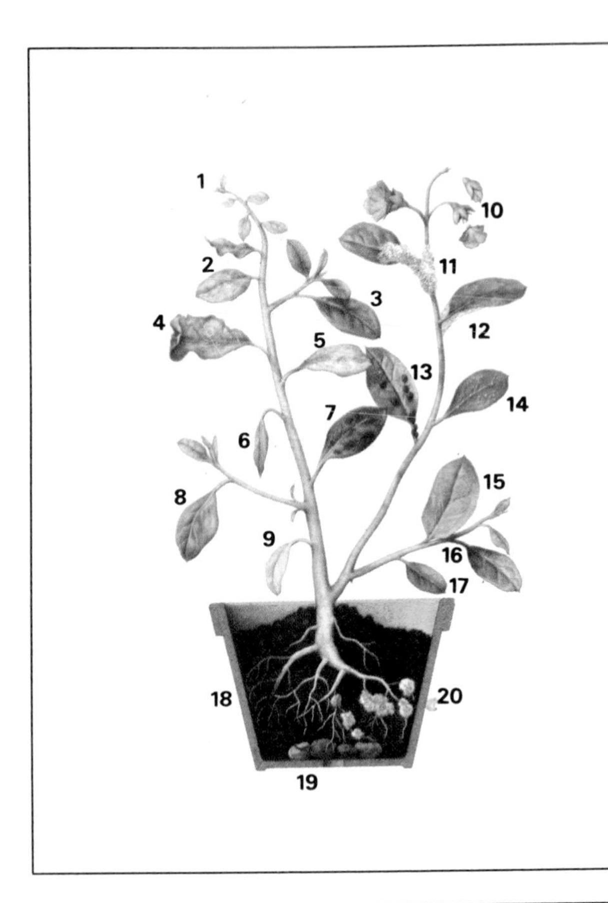

RULES FOR HEALTH

DO choose plants that will stand the average conditions of the room they're to live in.

DON'T let plants stand in a draft.

DON'T shut plants between curtains and windows on cold nights.

DON'T let strong sun scorch the plants—and keep sun off pots, too, or it will dry them out.

DON'T let hot dry air from radiators or other heaters get near delicate foliage.

DO keep room temperatures fairly even.

DO make sure there are no gas or oil fumes that can affect the plants.

Do make efforts to provide extra air moisture around your plants.

DON'T waterlog the soil, or let pots stand in water.

DON'T let the soil dry out completely.

DO avoid very cold water if possible.

DON'T water by the calendar—learn to test or feel the soil so that you know how much each plant needs.

DO water less in winter—most plants are "resting" then.

DO remember to feed plants regularly when they're growing actively, especially those in peat-based mixtures.

DON'T feed too often, or with too strong a solution.

DO clean plants regularly.

DO remember to repot plants when they need it; but don't keep looking at their roots!

SYMPTOMS

1 Weak spindly growth, with small, pale leaves.

2 Streaking and speckling of leaves.

3 Leaves that should be variegated stay green.

4 Green, brown, black or gray plant lice usually visible. Leaves yellowish, misshapen or not developing properly; little white "skeletons" on surface.

5 White "powder" on leaves.

6 Leaves all wilt or droop.

7 Brown scorched-looking patches or edges on leaves.

8 Yellow patches or edge markings on leaves.

9 Leaves turn yellow and then fall.

10 Buds and flowers drop too soon.

11 White "cotton-fuzz" on stem or leaf.

12 Leaf yellowish, often mottled; thin web on underside; tiny red or white specks.

13 Small, brown limpetlike objects on leaf surface or stems.

14 Tiny white insects, easily disturbed, usually on leaf undersides.

15 Leaves go yellow but stay on plant.

16 Rot on leaf or stem, or both.

17 Apparently healthy leaves fall.

18 Roots look soft and rotten.

19 Roots dried up.

20 White "absorbent-cotton" patches on roots.

IAGNOSIS	REMEDY
ack of light is usually the cause. When it occurs in inter, it's probably because the room is too warm. Warmth makes a plant grow when it should be "resting.")	Move to a brighter location, pinch back growing tips to encourage bushy growth and apply some plant fertilizer but not in winter.
ırips—minute jumping insects—are possible cause. They so attack flowers and can distort plant growth.	Wash leaves if light infestation. Spray with pyrethrum or malathion if heavy infestation.
ɔmetimes due to too little light. However, some plants, ıch a tradescantias can "revert" back to their plain-leafed ild-state form.	Move to brighter location. If whole shoot becomes plain green, nip it out.
ıese are aphids, which suck the plant's sap and cause aves to go yellow and finally to fall. Aphids excrete a veet "honeydew," which makes leaves sticky.	Wash leaves in clear water or soapy water (use household soap, not detergent), or spray with pyrethrum, rotenone, malathion or a systemic insecticide.
·obably mildew, a fungus disease often brought on by vermoist air, excess watering, and overcrowding.	Place plant in an airy location. Strictly ration the watering can and mister. Spray or dust with a sulfur fungicide.
sually the result of either lack of water or rotted roots here the soil has been overwatered and left airless and ggy. Other causes are exposure to hot sun, severe cold, exposure to gas fumes.	Check your watering habits. If necessary, de-pot and examine roots for rot. If overwatering is ruled out, move plant to better location.
arks may be due to many kinds of mistreatment—the ual one is hot dry air. Other possibilities are drafts, n scorch, overfeeding, overwatering, and water splashes at act as lenses when exposed to the sun.	Possibly a bad location for a plant. Move plant and check on your watering and fertilizing routine.
an be due to insect attack, but strong, blotchy marks are ually the result of too much plant fertilizer.	Reduce plant feeding. If marking is heavy, wash soil by pouring lots of clean water into top of pot and draining from bottom. This will wash out fertilizer in soil. Check also for possible insects in foliage and on stems.
aves will do this naturally from time to time, especially ar the base of the plant. If it happens to many leaves, eck for the following: overwatering, overfeeding, dry il, poor worn-out soil, drafts, either excessive cold or at, hot dry air, or gas fumes.	Go through checklist carefully and take appropriate action. If necessary, repot.
ıey can drop for reasons similar to those listed in (9). ıe most likely cause, however, is fluctuating temperatures. ɔme plants even drop buds if their pot is moved slightly.	It's usually too late to remedy. Try to find out the cause and take steps to ensure it doesn't happen again either to this or to your other plants.
sure sign of mealy bugs—insects that live protected from secticides in fuzzy covering. They suck plant juices.	Wash off with firm jet from hose or spray mister or paint them with alcohol, or spray with malathion.
ıspect spider mites, very small red or white pests just sible to the naked eye. If left undetected, spider mites ake a fine web under the leaf and around the leaf stem.	Separate from other plants as soon as discovered—mites spread quickly—wash with soapy water or spray forcibly, or apply sulfur dust, malathion or a systemic insecticide.
ıese are scale insects. The aphidlike creatures grow a ell and attach themselves permanently to leaves or stem.	Wash off with soapy water, looking carefully under all leaves. Spray with malathion or a systemic insecticide.
ıe miniature mothlike insects that fly out in masses when sturbed, are white fly. Adults and wingless larvae suck e plant juices.	Wash off with water jet or mist spray. Treat plant with malathion, rotenone, or pyrethrum. Very difficult to eradicate, so may need several applications.
:hlorosis" is probably the fault and is commonly caused lack of plant food. If symptoms appear in lime-hating ants, it means too much lime in the potting compost, or u're using hard water.	Try a magnesium-containing plant food or use "sequestered iron." If you have a water softener, don't water from an indoor faucet. Use rainwater or an outdoor faucet that bypasses the softener.
ually follows overwatering, especially in cold nditions. In some plants it could be caused by water dging between leaf and stem.	Check again on your watering routine. Though it's probably too late to save the affected plant, you'll avoid spreading the problem.
ant has had a shock. Suspect drafts, watering with cold ater, a violent change in temperature, gas fumes, cessive sun—or just dryness at the roots.	Go through the checklist to eliminate causes. Changing the location should help.
e soil is too wet, or you may be overfeeding the plant.	Reduce watering and strength of plant food.
is happens if the plant hasn't been watered enough.	Soak pot thoroughly, then drain. Misting may help.
a sign of root mealy bug.	Scrape away soil and inspect. If light infestation, water with malathion solution and repot in fresh soil.

Questions and Answers

Is it all right for me to remove the reddish covering around a new leaf on my rubber plant?
No. The sheath, as it's called, is nature's way of protecting a new leaf and you must let it fall off naturally in its own good time. That is when the leaf doesn't need it any more. Prying fingers might permanently damage the new leaf.

Patches of lighter and darker green have started to appear on the leaves of my rubber plant. Why is this? I'm not feeding the plant now, but I still water it once a week.
Something's gone wrong with the root system. You may have been overfeeding but it's more likely that you've overwatered. You shouldn't water any plant according to a fixed time schedule, but wait for the soil to become nearly dry and then fill the pot to the top, letting surplus water drain away. Try this method of watering, and start feeding again when the plant recovers.

Why do the leaves of my variegated ivies become plain green after I've had them for a time?
This is probably due to insufficient light. The best thing to do is cut out the all-green shoots or propagate from variegated pieces, and ensure that the plant is given plenty of light.

What can have happened? One or two of the leaves of my cissus vines have papery brown blotches on them. Are they too dry?
They're not too dry, they're sunburned. The trouble probably started when you watered and splashed the leaves when the plant was in full sunlight. A single drop of water on a leaf acts like a magnifying glass when the sun shines through it. Try to use a long-spouted watering pot so that you can direct the water onto the soil, only.

I'm very eager to grow house plants from seed. Is it possible, and if it is, where do I begin?
Many popular house plants are raised from seed. It isn't too difficult as long as you have the facilities for germinating seeds. A nice, constantly warm place, with a temperature of at least 65°F is vital for good results. You will also need plenty of well-lit space to cultivate your seedlings once they begin to grow. Packets of seeds can be bought at most nurseries with full growing instructions on them. It is very important to give the seedlings really good light (but not direct sunlight) once they have sprouted, and also to space them out well so they don't become overcrowded and spindly.

I was recently given a lovely container of mixed foliage and flowering plants. How can I best look after my instant indoor garden?
You may find after a month or two that the flowering plants are past their best. Take out the old plants and either replace them with other, similar plants or fill the gap with fresh soil. Be sure that you don't water the soil into a soggy mess as these decorative bowls don't usually have any drainage holes in them. Later on the foliage plants will probably start crowding each other; then you'll have to empty the bowl to thin out the plants and perhaps give the bigger plants separate pots.

Is it safe for me to repot my house plants in ordinary garden soil?
There's no such thing as "ordinary" garden soil. It varies enormously from district to district. The soil in even your neighbor's garden may be totally different to yours. Not only is garden soil often too heavy and dense but it can also contain harmful germs and

insects. Stick to using prepackaged soil mixes, which are sterilized.

I was given a lovely solanum plant, covered with big bright red berries. Having had it some weeks now the fruits are falling off quite rapidly. Why is this, and will it grow some more?
An occasional fall of berries is quite usual and natural but when almost all fall at once it probably means that your plant has been too hot and dry, or perhaps the soil dried out. Ideally it should be kept fairly cool and moist and well away from drafts and gas fumes. Unfortunately, it won't produce more berries this season but if you prune it fairly hard and place it out in the garden for the summer, you should have a good crop of berries for next winter.

My aechmea seems to have developed what looks to me like a white fungus in the "vase" part of the rosette. Have I overwatered for this to happen? I've kept it filled with water according to the nurseryman's instructions. Could something harmful have been in the water itself?
This "fungus" is only the calcareous deposits left by "hard" water from your faucet. Try to collect rainwater to put into your bromeliads.

The cuttings I took from a friend's big-leaved tradescantia were dark crimson, but now they are established, plain green leaves have started to sprout. What have I done wrong?
Your friend's plant (it could be either *Tradescantia blossfeldiana* or *Zebrina pendula*) was probably kept dry and in a hot, sunny place, which would account for the strong leaf color. You may be giving the cuttings too much water and food in comparison. You'll have to be harder on the plant to get the same results as your friend. The small-leaved *Tradescantia fluminensis*, with cream or pink markings, often "reverts" to pure green and such shoots should be cut right out, or they will "swamp" the rest of the plant.

I have a very pretty blue-flowered primula but whenever I touch it I get a red spotty rash; does this happen to everyone or am I unique?
The plant you mention is *Primula obconica*, which also comes with pink or red flowers and does give many people who touch it a rash or red "freckles." It is, fortunately, the only primula to cause this allergy. The only remedy is either not to touch it or to wear gloves when you have to—or grow the fairy primrose, *P. malacoides*, instead.

Whatever I do, the tips of the leaves of my palms, spider plants and some others go brown and dry. What can I do about this?
This is due to dry atmosphere and is almost impossible to prevent however much you provide extra humidity for your plants. It often happens even in fairly moist greenhouse conditions. Snip off the brown tips with scissors to improve the appearance of the long leaves.

Some of my plants collapsed and when I tipped out the soil in the pot I found a number of white grubs. Later on, I found black beetle-like insects with snouts wandering about. What are these and how can I prevent them?
This must be the vine weevil, which apart from vines can ruin begonias and cyclamens and will attack almost any house plant. The adult "beetles" are best picked up and destroyed individually, although most insecticide sprays will kill them. Water all the plants in the area with an insecticide solution made up as if for spraying. A solution of rotenone will usually kill the grubs, but one containing carbaryl is the most effective. You can mix carbaryl or rotenone into the potting soil when you are repotting.

My rubber plant is about to reach the ceiling and I want to stop it growing. What can I do?
You can't actually stop a rubber plant, or other strong tree-like house plant, from

growing. The only thing to do, however ruthless it may sound, is to cut it back. Cut it quite a long way down, because it will sprout again below that point. You can't use the top of the rubber plant like an ordinary cutting, it just won't root. If you want to make a brand new plant, carry out what is called air layering. To make an air layer, cut out a ring of bark about half an inch wide at the point where you want roots to form. Make two parallel cuts and peel the bark between them away very carefully. Dust this cut with a hormone root-forming powder if possible. Then, bind a large handful of moist sphagnum moss or coarse peat around the area of the ring, using a few turns of thread. Then surround this with plastic (use a plastic bag cut open), overlapping it well and tying the plastic firmly top and bottom. A few weeks later roots will show through the moss. The stem can then be cut below the moss ball, the moss carefully picked away, and the new plant potted up, making sure it is supported until the roots are long enough to hold it. Keep the old plant in the original pot and on the dry side until new shoots start sprouting.

I've heard of hydroponics—what does this mean?

Hydroponics means the growing of plants in water rather than soil—water to which liquid fertilizer is regularly added. It has been practiced for many years, and is an effective way of growing plants in desert areas where there is no proper soil. Many carnation growers use hydroponics regularly. There are several hydroponics systems; one of the latest in Europe has the plants growing in pebble-sized granules of expanded clay that has been

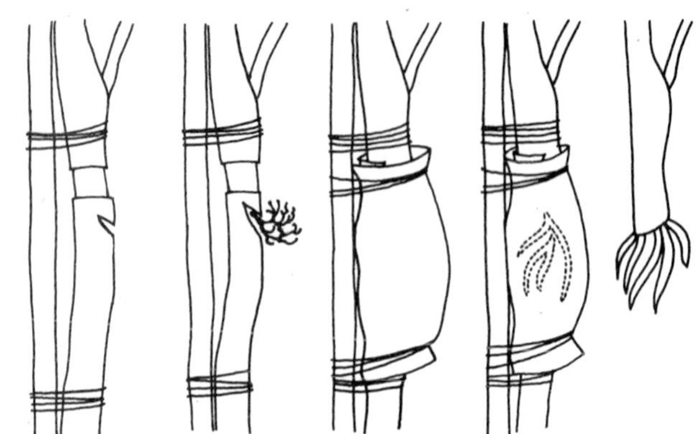

Above: Carrying out air layering on a leggy plant. **From left to right:** Either remove a band of bark all around the stem or make a small nick in the stem using a sharp knife (both methods are shown here). Then apply hormone rooting powder. If the nick method is used, keep the nick open by pushing a little sphagnum moss into it. Next, bind a handful of damp sphagnum moss around the cut area and cover it with a piece of plastic tied very firmly top and bottom. When roots can be seen through the plastic, unpack the layer and sever the stem below the roots.

Below: In hydroponics, plants are grown without soil. In the modern method shown, the roots are fed with a weak solution of fertilizer and supported in clay granules. The system is ideal for plants in offices or shop displays that may be left unattended for long periods.

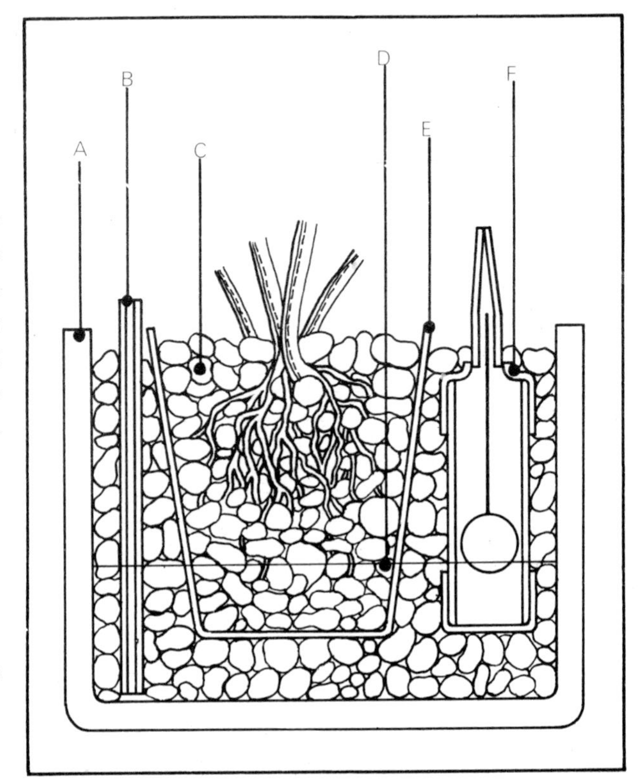

KEY
A Container
B Fertilizer and water input tube
C Clay granules
D Water level
E Perforated Pot
F Water level indicator

baked, complete with gauges to indicate the water level. But plants have been grown successfully in sand, vermiculite, perlite, or simply with the roots placed within containers or wire netting, suspended in a nutrient solution. It is, however, important to obtain a fertilizer solution specially made for hydroponic culture.

Something similar to hydroponics is the use of wicks. A wick, usually made of glass fiber, is pushed up through the bottom hole of a clay or china pot and teased out around it before the soil is put in. The lower end of the wick hangs down into a matching container in which water is placed.

Such methods are specially valuable in offices where the plants don't get much attention, and of course are a wonderful way of making sure your plants will stay happy when you're away on vacation.

I have had a poinsettia for a couple of years; it grows beautifully but I can't get it to flower and produce those lovely red leaves at Christmas.

You're up against something few people suspect—the poinsettia, like chrysanthemums and some other plants, is sensitive to the amount of daylight it gets. It is called a short-day plant, which means it won't flower if it gets more than around 12 hours light each day. Ordinary indoor lighting is quite enough to stop it flowering; so is light from a street lamp coming in at night. To make it flower you'll have to put it away every night from October onward in a dark closet or similar place.

My shrimp plant flowered all summer and now the bracts are beginning to fall off and some of the leaves are going brown. What has caused this and can I start again with cuttings?

It's quite usual for this to happen in the fall. Now is just the time of year to prune it into good shape and to take cuttings, which you can plant in good potting mix. When growing conditions are cold and wet the leaves have a tendency to change color and drop, but unless this is excessive don't worry about it. When the plant has finished flowering keep the compost fairly dry until next spring, when you can begin watering more freely.

Why won't my Christmas cactus flower? It keeps making lots of leaves but never any flowers.

See that the plant is in bright light and make sure the soil is moist during the year up until fall. In fall, change the routine. Reduce watering, keeping the soil on the dry side, but don't let it dry out completely.

When buds have developed, increase the water and fertilize every 10 days throughout the flowering period. Don't move the plant once it has buds or they may fall off. Follow all this and you should be rewarded with a flower-covered plant.

I had a very attractive aphelandra, but it has recently become covered with brownish limpet-like objects, which stick all over the leaves and stems. What are they and how can I get rid of them?

They are scale insects, sap-suckers that live under armored shells and are resistant to most ordinary insecticides. Dose your plant with a special systemic insecticide that will get into the sap stream and kill the insects as they feed on the sap. Alternatively, if you're very patient, you can sponge them off with a warm soapy solution.

I had a lovely flowering azalea during Christmas and I'm very unwilling to throw it out. Is it possible to keep it going?

It's not difficult, but takes a bit of trouble. Once the flowers are over, find a cool, frost-free place in very good light. Keep the pot soil just moist, but never let it dry out. Later, new shoots should appear, and you can repot it into a pot a size larger than the one it is in, using a potting mixture of equal parts peat, leafmold, and coarse sand. Don't use a prepackaged mix because they are usually too limy for azaleas. When there is no likelihood of more spring frosts place the pot outside, in a lightly shaded place, burying it if possible up to its rim. If you haven't a garden, find the coolest place in the house. Feed every fortnight, using a seaweed-based fertilizer if possible, and mist after hot days. Before the fall frosts, move the plant indoors and continue to keep it cool and in bright light but out of strong sun. Stop feeding and water lightly until flower buds appear, when more water can be given. Never put the plant in a hot dry atmosphere.

A few years ago I split up my very large aspidistra into five smaller plants. Three of them have large, dark green leaves but the other two have small, very pale ones. Why should they be so different?
The weak plants are probably part of the original, rather old worn-out clump. I suggest that you throw them away, for there is nothing you can do for them. Enjoy the three healthy ones instead.

When is the best time to repot a Christmas cactus? Should I divide it or take cuttings?
Early spring is usually the best time for dividing and repotting Christmas cactus. Divide the plant and put the rooted portions into pots of sandy, porous soil, rich in leaf mold. Cuttings of two or three of the leaflike stem segments, taken soon after the plant has flowered, will root very quickly if pushed for about ½ inch into a pot of sandy peat. Place cutting pots on a windowsill that isn't too bright, water them and cover with a clear plastic bag until they show signs of growing.

In my sun room I have a seven-foot high bougainvillea. As far as I can tell it's happy and healthy, so why are some of the leaves curling up and falling off?
It's behaving quite naturally. Bougainvilleas are inclined to shed leaves in winter—the end of their annual growth cycle. Keep the soil on the dry side and the temperature at about 50–55°F. In early spring, trim it to shape by shortening the shoots that flowered the previous year to within an inch of the older wood. Check its roots at the same time, too. It may have grown so much last season that it's now pot-bound. If it is, repot.

Should I let my maidenhair fern die down? Last year it did so of its own accord.
You don't need to force it to die down. If it does so naturally cut off the fronds to within about an inch of the crown to encourage new growth, and keep the soil only just moist.

I have an African violet that has become very bushy and big. Can I safely divide the plant up? And when is the best time to do this?
You can divide your plant almost any time when it is not in flower, though the very best time is in early spring. Water the plant well before taking it from the old pot. Gently ease the roots apart and carefully repot the separate plants into small pots of a peaty mixture. After potting, moisten the soil with tepid water and then keep them a bit on the dry side until it's obvious that they have grown a little. Then you can water normally.

Some time ago I planted some African violet leaves in a small pot of peaty soil mix, after rooting them in water. They're pretty healthy but there's no sign of shoots. What can I do?
Rooted leaves can take quite a long time to send up shoots. You'll have to be very patient. Encourage growth by putting the pot in a warm and moist place such as the bathroom or by the kitchen sink. If nothing happens in about three months' time you'll have to try again.

Whenever I cut back my poinsettia it drips a sticky white sap all over the place. How can I best stop this happening?
You can stop the sap flow by dusting the cuts with powdered charcoal or cool cigarette ash. Incidentally, the sap, or latex, should be kept well away from eyes or cut fingers as it stings horribly and can be quite dangerous.

I've heard about foliar feeding. How does it work?

Although the main way plants take in mineral food is through the roots, research has shown that they can also absorb it quite readily through the leaves. Foods absorbed in this way are very quickly taken into the plant's system. Modern foliar feeds not only contain the three basic growth elements (nitrogen, phosphorus, and potassium) but "trace" elements (those like iron and magnesium, required in very small amounts) and sometimes vitamins. Such foliar feeds are claimed to increase shoot and root growth, encourage earlier flowering where applicable, and to have a general tonic effect.

Since foliar feeding involves spraying the leaves with a fine mist, it is not as easy to apply indoors as a standard liquid feed watered into the pot. It can, however, easily be done at "maintenance time," when plants are often grouped together in a bath tub or sink, or can be taken outside to be sprayed over to wash off dirt and protect against pests.

What plants can I grow in a windowless bathroom?

None! No plant will endure many hours without light, and the hour or two the bathroom is likely to be illuminated each day is not enough to keep plants alive. Even if you kept the light on all the time, this would not be sufficient unless you have fluorescent tubes. If you really want some plants in a dark bathroom, we suggest you make a plant cabinet—or better still build it into a wall recess if possible—which has fluorescent tubes installed in it 18–24 inches above the plants. With this you could grow many plants, a lovely array of African violets for example. The lights would need to be on at least 15 hours a day.

Is rainwater lime-free?

Yes: rainwater cannot contain lime, and is normally very pure and clean. By using it you will also avoid chlorine, found in many town water supplies, and the excess iron that sometimes occurs. However, in industrial areas rainwater can contain sulfur dioxide and other chemicals that are carried into the air in smoke, as well as those chemicals deposited on the roofs from which the rainwater is collected. Such chemicals can sometimes be harmful to plants.

Why do plant roots rot in very wet soil whereas cuttings can produce roots in water and thrive?

Firstly, roots need oxygen to develop and live. Between the particles in ordinary soil, there are many gaps that hold air. Even in peat-based, soilless compounds the nature of the material is such that a good deal of air is retained in it. When soil or potting mixture are totally sodden, however, all the air is driven out and it is very difficult for it to return. In such conditions roots literally drown.

In a container of normal water there is a great deal of dissolved oxygen, and more is obtained from the air above it. However, the roots formed by cuttings in water are usually very fleshy, because they have large air spaces between the cells in order to cope with the problem. Such roots should be put into potting mixture with care, because they are rather brittle.

My begonia (a fibrous-rooted, stem-forming kind) apparently suffered during a long vacation we took, and all but one shoot died. The one shoot is at the edge of the pot and is now, after loving attention, thriving, but it looks pretty peculiar, stuck off at the side. Should I repot it, and if so, should it go in a smaller pot?

It should be quite safe now to do as you suggest with the surviving begonia shoot. Take it carefully out of the present pot and you will probably find that much of the soil on the side away from the plant will fall away, having no root in it. Find a new pot of the right size to hold what roots remain—it will probably be a bit smaller—and carefully repot. These begonias typically produce new shoots from the base.

Picture Credits

The authors and publishers gratefully acknowledge the following individuals for giving permission to reprint their photographs.

Key (b) bottom, (c) center, (l) left, (r) right, (t) top

Bernard Alfieri: 70 (all), 171 (cl)
A–Z Botanical Collection: 31 (br), 32, 33, (cl, br), 41 (tr), 47 (tc), 50, 87, 97 (br), 98 (bl)
Pat Brindley: 28 (bl), 29 (tl, tc, bl), 31 (tc), 33 (tr), 37 (bl, br), 40 (b), 40–1 (c), 41 (br), 42, 45 (bl, br), 47 (cc), 52–3 (t), 56, 58 (bl), 66 (t), 69, 71 (tl), 74, 81 (tl), 83, 93 (t), 122–3
Camera Press: 101 (tr)
R. J. Corbin: 118 (t)
Brian Furner: 118 (bl, br), 119
Susan Griggs Agency (Michael Boys, photographer): 4, 6, 27 (tr, br), 35 (tl), 39, 43, 44 (l), 46, 47 (tl), 51 (br), 81 (br), 98 (t)
Harry Smith Horticultural Photographic Collection: 27 (tl, cl, cr), 28 (br), 29 (tr, cl), 33 (tl, bl), 34, 35 (cr), 37 (tl, tr), 40 (tl), 45 (tl), 47 (cr), 51 (bl), 52 (tl, bl, bc, br), 53 (b), 56–7 (bc), 57 (br), 58 (br), 59 (t, b), 64 (bl), 66 (c, b), 67 (all), 71 (tr, br), 76, 77 (l, r), 84–5 (all), 89, 90–1 (all), 97 (bl, bc)
Syndication International: 102–3
Elizabeth Whiting Agency: 49, 101 (tl)

The following photographs were taken by the authors in their own home: 20 (bl), 28 (t), 30, 31 (tl, tr, bl, bc), 33 (bc), 35 (tr, br), 36, 38, 44 (tr), 45 (tr), 47 (br), 64 (t), 75, 79, 80 (all), 91 (tr), 93 (b), 99 (b), 101 (bl), 103 (r), 104–5 (all), 110 (tr), 111, 112–3, 114–5 (all), 120 (b), 124–5 (all), 126 (all), 129 (all), 131

Any photographs not credited above were commissioned by the publishers especially for HUXLEY'S HOUSE OF PLANTS. Among the contributing photographers were: George Adams, Michael Boys, and Eric Crichton.

Index

Page numbers in italics denote illustrations.